SLOW

Cooker

throw it in and let it simmer

MURDOCH BOOKS

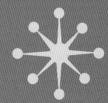

Imagine coming home to a kitchen full of heavenly aromas and a flavoursome meal simmering away just begging to be eaten. Enter the slow cooker. This simple kitchen appliance has come into its own as home cooks rediscover its ability to transform basic ingredients into comforting meals — all while you shop, work, play or even sleep. Another great advantage is that slow cookers often work best with cheaper cuts of meat, making these meals low in price as well as effort. Pick your mood and choose from family favourites, spicy surprises and wonderfully indulgent dinner party dishes. Welcome to the magical world of the slow cooker.

Contents

Family

Hearty chicken noodle soup • Sweet and sour braised pork • Beef and vegetable stew • Chicken, pumpkin and honey braise • Vegetable and gnocchi stew • Lasagne with ham, lemon and basil • Chinese chicken with almonds and lemon • Pork with apple sauce • Creamy meatballs • Chicken with satay sauce • Rosemary and redcurrant lamb roast • Sticky pork ribs • Corn and crab soup • Lamb ragù • Mexican chicken • Pork with succotash • Lamb meatballs with spicy saffron sauce • Marmalade-glazed corned beef • Beef short ribs with molasses, bourbon and thyme • Cajun chicken stew • Cream of parsnip soup • Veal cacciatore • Chinese braised lamb • Braised teriyaki beef with udon noodles • Bacon-wrapped pork cooked with maple syrup • Greek lamb with risoni and feta • Spanish chicken • Savoury mince • Abruzzi-style lamb

☀ Preparation time: 15 minutes   **☀ Cooking time:** 7 hours   **☀ Serves:** 4–6

Hearty chicken noodle soup

800 g (1 lb 12 oz) chicken breast fillets
500 ml (17 fl oz/2 cups) good-quality
    chicken stock
2 celery stalks, diced
1 onion, diced
2 carrots, peeled and diced
1 parsnip, peeled and diced
2 cm (¾ inch) piece of fresh ginger
3 black peppercorns
220 g (7¾ oz) fresh rice noodles
2 zucchini (courgettes), diced
1 handful parsley, finely chopped

Place the chicken, stock, celery, onion, carrot, parsnip, ginger, peppercorns and 250 ml (9 fl oz/1 cup) water in a slow cooker. Cover and cook on low for 6 hours.

Remove the chicken fillets from the slow cooker and allow to cool slightly. When cool enough to handle, shred the chicken into bite-sized pieces.

Return the shredded chicken to the slow cooker and stir in the noodles and zucchini. Turn the slow cooker setting to high and cook for a further 1 hour.

Discard the ginger and season to taste with sea salt and freshly ground black pepper. Ladle the soup into deep serving bowls. Sprinkle with the parsley and serve.

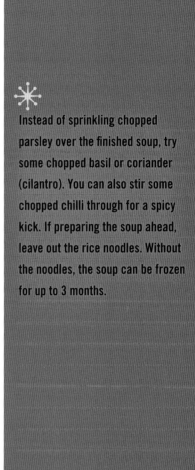

Instead of sprinkling chopped parsley over the finished soup, try some chopped basil or coriander (cilantro). You can also stir some chopped chilli through for a spicy kick. If preparing the soup ahead, leave out the rice noodles. Without the noodles, the soup can be frozen for up to 3 months.

Sweet and sour braised pork

If you have time, refrigerate the cooked braised pork mixture overnight. The fat will set in a layer on top of the stew, making it easy to skim off. Gently reheat the stew, adding a little water to loosen the mixture if needed. The flavour will also intensify if refrigerated overnight.

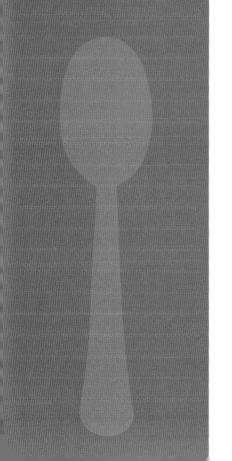

8 pork spare ribs (pork belly), about 1.25 kg (2 lb 12 oz) in total
½ small pineapple, about 500 g (1 lb 2 oz), peeled and cored, then chopped into 2 cm (¾ inch) pieces
1 carrot, peeled and thickly sliced
1 red onion, roughly chopped
400 g (14 oz/2 cups) jasmine rice
2 spring onions (scallions), chopped on the diagonal, to garnish
1 long red chilli, sliced, to garnish

Soy marinade
2 teaspoons cornflour (cornstarch)
1 teaspoon sea salt
60 ml (2 fl oz/¼ cup) Chinese rice wine
2 tablespoons tomato sauce (ketchup)
2 tablespoons soy sauce
1 tablespoon grated palm sugar (jaggery)

In a large bowl, combine the soy marinade ingredients. Mix well to dissolve the sugar, then add the pork and toss to coat. Cover and marinate in the refrigerator overnight.

The next day, transfer the pork to a slow cooker. Add the pineapple, carrot and onion, then cover and cook on low for 8 hours.

Meanwhile, near serving time, prepare the rice. Rinse the rice under cold running water until the water runs clear. Place the rice in a saucepan with 450 ml (16 fl oz) water. Bring to the boil and boil for 1 minute. Cover tightly, reduce the heat to as low as possible and cook for 10 minutes. Remove from the heat and leave to stand, covered, for 10 minutes.

Spoon the rice onto serving plates or into wide shallow bowls, then ladle the pork mixture over the top. Garnish with the spring onion and chilli slices and serve.

Preparation time: 10 minutes
plus overnight marinating

Cooking time: 8 hours

Serves: 4

Preparation time: 25 minutes   **Cooking time:** 4 hours   **Serves:** 4

Beef and vegetable stew

1 onion
1 carrot
1 parsnip
1 swede (rutabaga) or turnip
2 all-purpose potatoes
250 g (9 oz) sweet potato
1 celery stalk
100 g (3½ oz) button mushrooms
2 thick rindless bacon slices,
  roughly chopped
1 kg (2 lb 4 oz) beef blade, skirt steak
  or chuck steak, cut into 4 cm
  (1½ inch) chunks
2 garlic cloves, chopped
1 teaspoon dried oregano
400 ml (14 fl oz) good-quality beef
  or chicken stock
400 g (14 oz) tin chopped tomatoes
2 tablespoons tomato paste
  (concentrated purée)
60 ml (2 fl oz/¼ cup) red wine
1 small handful flat-leaf (Italian)
  parsley, chopped

Peel the onion, carrot, parsnip, swede, potatoes and sweet potato and cut into 4 cm (1½ inch) chunks. Cut the celery into 4 cm (1½ inch) chunks. Wipe the mushrooms clean and slice in half.

Put the vegetables in a slow cooker with the bacon and beef. Scatter the garlic and oregano over.

In a bowl, mix together the stock, tomatoes, tomato paste and wine, then pour over the beef mixture. Season well with sea salt and freshly ground black pepper.

Cover and cook on high for 4 hours, or until the meat and vegetables are tender.

Ladle into serving bowls, sprinkle with the parsley and serve.

This stew is delicious served with steamed green or yellow beans and good crusty bread.

Chicken, pumpkin and honey braise

Honey mustard, as its name suggests, is a ready-made condiment containing honey and mustard. The mustard used in it is generally mild, but can vary in tang and spiciness, with the honey contributing a mellow sweetness. Honey mustard can be used in salad dressings, glazes, meat marinades or as a dipping sauce, but if you don't have any, you can just use wholegrain mustard in this recipe.

750 g (1 lb 10 oz) butternut pumpkin (squash), peeled, seeded and chopped into 2.5 cm (1 inch) chunks
1 large onion, chopped
1 kg (2 lb 4 oz) skinless chicken thigh fillets
2 tablespoons honey
2 tablespoons honey mustard
250 ml (9 fl oz/1 cup) good-quality chicken stock
400 g (14 oz/2 cups) basmati rice
2 tablespoons chopped flat-leaf (Italian) parsley

Place the pumpkin and onion in a slow cooker, then arrange the chicken on top.

In a bowl, mix together the honey, mustard and stock, then pour over the chicken.

Cover and cook on high for 3 hours.

Meanwhile, near serving time, prepare the rice. Rinse the rice under cold running water until the water runs clear. Place the rice and 375 ml (13 fl oz/1½ cups) cold water in a large saucepan, then cover and cook over low heat for 20–25 minutes, or until the rice is tender.

Just before serving, stir half the parsley through the chicken mixture.

Spoon the rice onto serving plates or into wide shallow bowls. Ladle the chicken braise over the top, sprinkle with the remaining parsley and serve.

Preparation time: 15 minutes   **Cooking time:** 8 hours   **Serves:** 4

Vegetable and gnocchi stew

1 onion, chopped

3 garlic cloves, chopped

2 zucchini (courgettes), cut into
  2 cm (¾ inch) dice

1 red capsicum (pepper), trimmed,
  seeded and cut into 2 cm (¾ inch) dice

100 g (3½ oz) button mushrooms

500 g (1 lb 2 oz) fresh gnocchi

600 ml (21 fl oz) jar tomato passata
  (puréed tomatoes)

500 ml (17 fl oz/2 cups) good-quality
  chicken stock

125 ml (4 fl oz/½ cup) white wine

2 rosemary sprigs

1 small handful chopped basil, plus
  extra sprigs, to garnish

100 g (3½ oz/1 cup) shaved parmesan

Place the onion, garlic, zucchini, capsicum and mushrooms in a slow cooker. Arrange the gnocchi over the top.

In a bowl, mix together the passata, stock and wine. Pour the mixture into the slow cooker, but do not stir as the gnocchi are quite fragile. Add the rosemary sprigs.

Cover and cook on low for 8 hours.

Season to taste with sea salt and freshly ground black pepper and gently stir the basil through.

Ladle into serving bowls and scatter the parmesan over the top. Garnish with extra basil sprigs and serve.

For a vegetarian version of this dish, use vegetable stock instead of chicken stock. For non-vegetarians, you could also gently stir 200 g (7 oz) chopped ham through the stew when adding the basil. To vary the recipe a little, swap the parmesan for dollops of fresh ricotta, if desired.

Lasagne with ham, lemon and basil

Instead of shredded ham, try using chopped prosciutto, and replace the cheddar cheese with mozzarella. For a vegetarian meal, simply omit the ham or prosciutto altogether. When assembling the lasagne layers, break the instant lasagne sheets to fit the shape of the slow cooker.

olive oil, for brushing
690 ml (24 fl oz) jar tomato passata (puréed tomatoes)
2 garlic cloves, crushed
150 g (5½ oz/1¼ cups) grated cheddar cheese
50 g (1¾ oz/½ cup) grated parmesan
1 egg
300 ml (10½ fl oz) thick cream
1 handful basil, chopped
1 teaspoon grated lemon rind
150 g (5½ oz) shaved ham, shredded
250 g (9 oz) packet instant lasagne sheets
mixed salad leaves, to serve

Lightly brush the bowl of a slow cooker with olive oil.

In a bowl, mix together the passata and garlic.

In a separate bowl, mix together 125 g (4½ oz/1 cup) of the cheddar, the parmesan, egg, cream, basil and lemon rind. Season to taste with sea salt and freshly ground black pepper.

Spoon one-third of the passata mixture into the slow cooker. Top with one-third of the ham and one-quarter of the cheese mixture. Arrange one-third of the lasagne sheets over the top in a single layer.

Spoon another one-third of the passata mixture over the lasagne sheets, then top with another one-third of the ham and one-quarter of the cheese mixture. Layer another one-third of the lasagne sheets over the top.

Repeat with the remaining passata, ham, another one-quarter of the cheese mixture and the remaining lasagne sheets to make a third layer.

Spread the remaining cheese mixture over the top of the lasagne, ensuring that all the pasta is covered, otherwise it will not cook through properly. Sprinkle with the remaining cheddar.

Cover and cook on low for 3 hours, or until the pasta is tender.

Allow the lasagne to sit for 10 minutes before serving with mixed salad leaves.

✳ **Preparation time:** 25 minutes   ✳ **Cooking time:** 3 hours   ✳ **Serves:** 4–6

Preparation time: 20 minutes ✳ **Cooking time:** 3 hours 30 minutes ✳ **Serves:** 4

Chinese chicken with almonds and lemon

2 celery stalks, thickly sliced
2 small carrots, peeled and
  thickly sliced
1 garlic clove, finely chopped
1 cm (½ inch) piece of fresh ginger,
  peeled and sliced into thin strips
375 ml (13 fl oz/1½ cups) good-quality
  chicken stock
1 tablespoon Chinese rice wine
1 teaspoon sesame oil
1 tablespoon cornflour (cornstarch)
2 tablespoons oyster sauce
60 ml (2 fl oz/¼ cup) soy sauce
1 teaspoon caster (superfine) sugar
1 tablespoon lemon juice
600 g (1 lb 5 oz) chicken breast fillets,
  thinly sliced
400 g (14 oz/2 cups) jasmine rice
45 g (1½ oz/½ cup) flaked almonds,
  toasted
thinly sliced spring onions (scallions),
  to garnish

Place the celery, carrot, garlic, ginger, stock, rice wine and sesame oil in a slow cooker. Cover and cook on high for 3 hours.

In a large bowl, mix together the cornflour, oyster sauce, soy sauce, sugar and lemon juice until the sugar has dissolved. Add the chicken slices and toss to coat.

Add the chicken and the sauce mixture to the slow cooker. Cover and cook for a further 30 minutes, or until the chicken is cooked through and the sauce has thickened.

Meanwhile, near serving time, prepare the rice. Rinse the rice under cold running water until the water runs clear. Place the rice in a saucepan with 450 ml (16 fl oz) water. Bring to the boil and boil for 1 minute. Cover tightly, reduce the heat to as low as possible and cook for 10 minutes. Remove from the heat and leave to stand, covered, for 10 minutes.

Spoon the rice onto serving plates or into wide shallow bowls, then ladle the chicken mixture over the top. Sprinkle with the almonds and spring onion and serve.

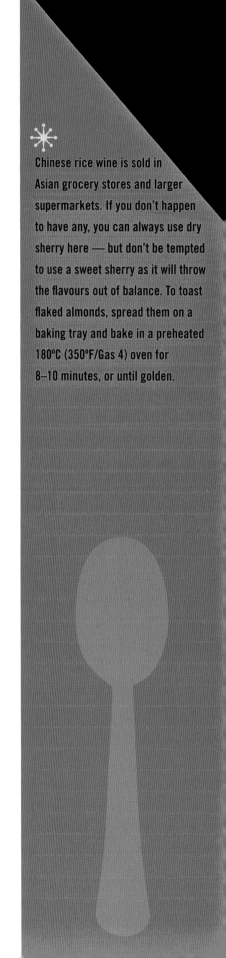

Chinese rice wine is sold in Asian grocery stores and larger supermarkets. If you don't happen to have any, you can always use dry sherry here — but don't be tempted to use a sweet sherry as it will throw the flavours out of balance. To toast flaked almonds, spread them on a baking tray and bake in a preheated 180°C (350°F/Gas 4) oven for 8–10 minutes, or until golden.

Pork with apple sauce

kg (2 lb 4 oz) boneless pork leg
roast, trimmed and cut into 4 cm
(1½ inch) chunks
1 tablespoon rosemary
1 leek, white part only, rinsed well,
trimmed and chopped
500 g (1 lb 2 oz) sweet potatoes, peeled
and cut into 3 cm (1¼ inch) chunks
1 small fennel bulb, trimmed and
thickly sliced
100 g (3½ oz) button mushrooms,
halved
1 apple, peeled, cored and chopped
2 garlic cloves, chopped
375 ml (13 fl oz/1½ cups) sparkling
apple cider
1 tablespoon cornflour (cornstarch)
2 tablespoons chopped flat-leaf
(Italian) parsley
steamed English spinach, to serve

Place the pork in a slow cooker. Sprinkle with the rosemary, season well with sea salt and freshly ground black pepper and gently toss to coat.

Add the leek, sweet potato, fennel, mushrooms, apple and garlic to the slow cooker and gently mix together. Pour in the cider.

Cover and cook on high for 5 hours, or until the pork is tender.

Remove the lid. Blend the cornflour with 1 tablespoon water until smooth, then stir through the pork mixture.

Cook, uncovered, for a further 15 minutes, or until the sauce has thickened slightly.

Sprinkle with the parsley and serve with steamed spinach.

Preparation time: 25 minutes ✳ **Cooking time:** 5 hours 15 minutes ✳ **Serves:** 4

Preparation time: 20 minutes · **Cooking time:** 4 hours 20 minutes · **Serves:** 4

Creamy meatballs

3 slices (60 g/2¼ oz) day-old crusty
  bread, crusts removed
185 ml (6 fl oz/¾ cup) milk
300 g (10½ oz) minced (ground) pork
300 g (10½ oz) minced (ground) beef
60 g (2¼ oz/¼ cup) grated onion
1 teaspoon sea salt flakes
1 teaspoon ground white pepper
1 teaspoon ground coriander seeds
¼ teaspoon ground allspice
2 tablespoons olive oil
125 ml (4 fl oz/½ cup) good-quality
  chicken stock
125 ml (4 fl oz/½ cup) cream
1 tablespoon chopped dill, plus extra,
  to garnish
finely grated rind of 1 lemon
sliced gherkins (pickles), to serve
  (optional)

Beetroot, orange and goat's cheese salad
440 g (15 oz) tin baby beetroot (beets)
  in juice, rinsed and drained
1 handful mixed salad leaves
1 blood orange, cut into segments, peel
  and all white pith removed
60 ml (2 fl oz/¼ cup) extra virgin olive oil
1½ tablespoons red wine vinegar
80 g (2¾ oz/⅔ cup) crumbled goat's
  cheese

Roughly chop the bread and place in a bowl. Pour the milk over and set aside to soften for 5 minutes. Squeeze out and discard most of the excess milk.

In a bowl, combine the bread, pork, beef, onion, sea salt flakes, white pepper, coriander and allspice and mix together well using your hands. Using clean wet hands, form the mixture into 24 meatballs, using about one heaped tablespoon of mixture per ball.

Heat half the olive oil in a large frying pan over medium–high heat. Add half the meatballs and fry for 3–4 minutes, or until golden all over, turning regularly. Remove to a slow cooker.

Heat the remaining oil in the pan and brown the remaining meatballs in the same way. Place in the slow cooker. Pour in the stock and cream.

Cover and cook on low for 3–4 hours, or until the meatballs are cooked through and tender.

Meanwhile, near serving time, make the beetroot, orange and goat's cheese salad. Wearing gloves, cut the beetroot into quarters and place in a bowl with the salad leaves and orange segments. Whisk together the olive oil and vinegar, season with sea salt and freshly ground black pepper and drizzle over the salad. Gently toss together, then crumble the goat's cheese over the top.

When the meatballs are cooked, strain the cooking juices into a large frying pan and place over high heat. Cook for 5–10 minutes, stirring regularly, until the liquid has reduced by half and the sauce is very tasty. Stir in the dill.

Divide the meatballs among serving plates or wide shallow bowls, then drizzle the sauce over the top. Sprinkle with the lemon rind and a little extra dill. Serve with the beetroot salad and gherkins, if desired.

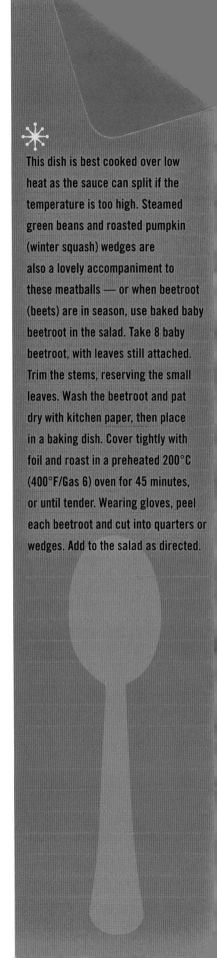

This dish is best cooked over low heat as the sauce can split if the temperature is too high. Steamed green beans and roasted pumpkin (winter squash) wedges are also a lovely accompaniment to these meatballs — or when beetroot (beets) are in season, use baked baby beetroot in the salad. Take 8 baby beetroot, with leaves still attached. Trim the stems, reserving the small leaves. Wash the beetroot and pat dry with kitchen paper, then place in a baking dish. Cover tightly with foil and roast in a preheated 200°C (400°F/Gas 6) oven for 45 minutes, or until tender. Wearing gloves, peel each beetroot and cut into quarters or wedges. Add to the salad as directed.

Chicken with satay sauce

8 chicken thigh fillets, about 1 kg
  (2 lb 4 oz), trimmed of excess fat
290 ml (10 fl oz) tin satay sauce
125 ml (4 fl oz/½ cup) coconut milk
400 g (14 oz/2 cups) jasmine rice
1 tablespoon toasted peanuts, chopped
90 g (3½ oz/1 cup) bean sprouts,
  tails trimmed
1 handful coriander (cilantro) sprigs

Soy and lemongrass marinade
2 teaspoons Thai red curry paste
4 garlic cloves, crushed
2 lemongrass stems, white part only,
  chopped
125 ml (4 fl oz/½ cup) soy sauce
1 tablespoon soft brown sugar

Combine the soy and lemongrass marinade ingredients in a food processor and blend until smooth. Place the chicken thighs in a bowl and pour the marinade over them, tossing to coat. Cover and marinate in the refrigerator overnight.

Transfer the chicken and the marinade to a slow cooker. Pour the satay sauce and coconut milk over.

Cover and cook on low for 6 hours.

Meanwhile, near serving time, prepare the rice. Rinse the rice under cold running water until the water runs clear. Place the rice in a saucepan with 450 ml (16 fl oz) water. Bring to the boil and boil for 1 minute. Cover tightly, reduce the heat to as low as possible and cook for 10 minutes. Remove from the heat and leave to stand, covered, for 10 minutes.

When the chicken is done, check the satay sauce for taste and season with sea salt if required. Remove the thighs to a chopping board using tongs or a slotted spoon. Thickly slice each chicken thigh.

Spoon the rice onto serving plates or into wide shallow bowls, then arrange the chicken over the top. Drizzle the chicken with the satay sauce. Garnish with the peanuts, bean sprouts and coriander and serve.

✳ **Preparation time:** 15 minutes
plus overnight marinating

✳ **Cooking time:** 6 hours

✳ **Serves:** 4

Preparation time: 20 minutes   **Cooking time:** 8 hours   **Serves:** 6

Rosemary and redcurrant lamb roast

2.25 kg (5 lb) leg of lamb, trimmed
  of excess fat
1 garlic clove, halved
3 rosemary sprigs, cut in half
160 g (5¾ oz/½ cup) redcurrant jelly,
  melted
½ small pumpkin (winter squash),
  about 650 g (1 lb 7 oz) in total
1 onion
12 new potatoes, about 900 g (2 lb)
  in total
1 bay leaf
1 tablespoon olive oil
steamed peas, to serve

Cut six large incisions into the lamb, then rub the lamb all over with the cut garlic. Insert the rosemary sprigs into the incisions. Brush the lamb well with half the redcurrant jelly and season generously with sea salt and freshly ground black pepper.

Leaving the skin on, remove the seeds from the pumpkin and cut the flesh into 5 cm (2 inch) wedges. Peel the onion and cut into rounds, but do not separate the rings. Scrub the potatoes but leave the skins on. Cut any larger ones in half.

Place the potatoes, pumpkin, onion and bay leaf in the slow cooker, then rest the lamb on top. Cover and cook on low for 8 hours.

Remove the lamb from the slow cooker and place on a warmed platter. Cover with foil and leave to rest in a warm place for 10 minutes before carving.

Drizzle the vegetables in the slow cooker with the olive oil and season to taste with sea salt and freshly ground black pepper.

Carve the lamb and divide among serving plates. Serve with the remaining redcurrant jelly, the braised vegetables and peas.

Instead of the pumpkin (winter squash), you can use 600 g (1 lb 5 oz) chopped sweet potato in this recipe. You can leave the skin on if you wish, but wash the sweet potato well before using.

Sticky pork ribs

olive oil, for brushing
1.25 kg (2 lb 12 oz) pork barbecue ribs
  (not spare ribs)
1 red onion, finely chopped
1 green capsicum (pepper), trimmed,
  seeded and finely chopped
1 green chilli, seeded and finely chopped
2 garlic cloves, finely chopped
185 ml (6 fl oz/¾ cup) barbecue sauce
2 tablespoons white wine vinegar
2 tablespoons soft brown sugar
1 tablespoon sweet chilli sauce
2 teaspoons worcestershire sauce
a dash of Tabasco sauce
coriander (cilantro) leaves, to garnish
  (optional)
trussed cherry tomatoes, to serve

Corn salsa
350 g (12 oz/2⅓ cups) frozen corn
  kernels
2 spring onions (scallions), finely
  chopped
1 tablespoon finely chopped coriander
  (cilantro) leaves
1 tablespoon extra virgin olive oil
2 tablespoons lime juice

Lightly brush the bowl of a slow cooker with olive oil. Cut the ribs into sets of two or three; trim off any excess fat.

Put the ribs in the slow cooker. Scatter the onion, capsicum, chilli and garlic over the ribs. Season well with sea salt and freshly ground black pepper.

In a small bowl, combine the barbecue sauce, vinegar, sugar, chilli sauce, worcestershire sauce, Tabasco and 60 ml (2 fl oz/¼ cup) water. Mix well to dissolve the sugar, then pour over the ribs.

Cover and cook on high for 3½ hours, or until the ribs are tender. During cooking, stir the mixture once or twice to keep the ribs covered with the sauce.

After 3½ hours, check the ribs — the meat should be tender, but not falling off the bone. If the meat isn't yet tender, put the lid back on and continue to cook for another 30 minutes.

Meanwhile, near serving time, prepare the corn salsa. Bring a saucepan of water to the boil over high heat. Add the corn and cook for 2–3 minutes, or until just tender. Drain well, then place in a bowl. Add the spring onion, coriander, olive oil and lime juice and gently toss to combine.

Using tongs, remove the ribs to a large serving plate. Skim off any surface fat from the sauce, then spoon some sauce over the ribs. Garnish with coriander if desired. Serve with the corn salsa and cherry tomatoes.

Preparation time: 20 minutes   **Cooking time:** 4 hours   **Serves:** 4–6

Preparation time: 10 minutes　　　**Cooking time:** 2 hours　　　**Serves:** 4

Corn and crab soup

420 g (15 oz) tin creamed corn

2 teaspoons grated fresh ginger

2 x 170 g (6 oz) tins crabmeat

6 spring onions (scallions), trimmed and sliced thinly on the diagonal, plus extra, to garnish

750 ml (26 fl oz/3 cups) good-quality chicken stock

1 tablespoon mirin

2 tablespoons soy sauce, plus extra, to serve

¼ teaspoon ground white pepper

2 egg whites, lightly beaten

Place the corn, ginger, crabmeat and half the spring onion in a slow cooker. Pour in the stock, mirin and 500 ml (17 fl oz/2 cups) water.

Cover and cook on low for 2 hours.

Stir in the soy sauce and white pepper. Add the egg whites and remaining spring onion and stir for 1–2 minutes, or until the egg has just cooked through.

Ladle the soup into serving bowls and sprinkle with extra spring onion. Serve immediately, with extra soy sauce on the side.

Mirin is a Japanese cooking wine. If unavailable, you can substitute Chinese rice wine or dry sherry in this recipe. It's important not to let the egg cook too long in this soup — serve it straight away, while the egg is still velvety and soft.

Lamb ragù

1 kg (2 lb 4 oz) minced (ground) lamb
400 g (14 oz) tin chopped tomatoes
250 ml (9 fl oz/1 cup) tomato passata
  (puréed tomatoes) or pasta sauce
125 ml (4 fl oz/½ cup) red wine
2 carrots, peeled and diced
2 onions, diced
2 celery stalks, diced
2 tablespoons pesto
2 tablespoons tomato paste
  (concentrated purée)
4 garlic cloves, crushed
1 teaspoon chilli flakes
½ teaspoon dried oregano
1 rosemary sprig
1 thyme sprig
400 g (14 oz) pasta tubes, such as
  penne or rigatoni
1 small handful finely chopped flat-leaf
  (Italian) parsley
50 g (1¾ oz/½ cup) finely grated
  parmesan

Put the lamb, tomatoes and passata in a slow cooker. Pour in the wine, then add the carrot, onion, celery, pesto, tomato paste and garlic. Sprinkle with the chilli flakes and oregano and add the rosemary and thyme sprigs.

Cover and cook on low for 5½ hours.

Meanwhile, near serving time, add the pasta to a large pot of rapidly boiling salted water and cook according to the packet instructions until al dente, about 10 minutes. Drain well.

Divide the pasta among serving bowls, then spoon the lamb ragù over the top. Sprinkle with the parsley and parmesan and serve.

✳ Preparation time: 15 minutes **✳ Cooking time:** 5 hours 30 minutes **✳ Serves:** 4–6

Preparation time: 20 minutes **Cooking time:** 6 hours 20 minutes **Serves:** 4

Mexican chicken

1 tablespoon chilli flakes
2 teaspoons ground cumin
¼ teaspoon ground cinnamon
60 ml (2 fl oz/¼ cup) olive oil
1.25 kg (2 lb 12 oz) chicken pieces,
  skin on
1 red onion, finely chopped
2 green jalapeño chillies, finely chopped
4 garlic cloves, finely chopped
200 ml (7 fl oz) hot taco sauce
125 ml (4 fl oz/½ cup) good-quality
  chicken stock
1 red capsicum (pepper), trimmed,
  seeded and chopped into 2 cm
  (¾ inch) chunks
1 green capsicum (pepper), trimmed,
  seeded and chopped into 2 cm
  (¾ inch) chunks
2 corn cobs, silks and husks removed,
  each cut into thick rounds
400 g (14 oz/2 cups) basmati rice
100 g (3½ oz) whole black olives
1 small handful coriander (cilantro)
  leaves
80 g (2¾ oz/⅓ cup) sour cream
warmed flour tortillas, to serve
  (optional)

In a small bowl, mix together the chilli flakes, cumin, cinnamon and 2 tablespoons of the olive oil until well combined.

Place the chicken pieces in a large bowl, add the spice and oil mixture and toss to coat. Rub the spice mixture into the chicken skin with your fingers, making sure the chicken is entirely covered. Season with sea salt.

Heat the remaining oil in a large frying pan over medium heat. Add the chicken pieces in batches and fry for 10 minutes, turning occasionally, until the skin has browned, transferring each batch to a slow cooker.

Add the onion, jalapeño chilli, garlic, taco sauce, stock, capsicums and corn to the slow cooker. Mix well to ensure all the ingredients are evenly distributed.

Cover and cook on low for 6 hours.

Meanwhile, near serving time, prepare the rice. Rinse the rice under cold running water until the water runs clear. Place the rice and 375 ml (13 fl oz/1½ cups) cold water in a large saucepan, then cover and cook over low heat for 20–25 minutes, or until the rice is tender.

Stir the olives through the chicken mixture. Divide among serving plates and sprinkle with the coriander. Serve with the rice and sour cream, and warmed flour tortillas if desired.

Pork with succotash

Pancetta is the Italian name for cured pork belly. You'll find it in delicatessens and continental butcher's stores. If pancetta is unavailable, use good-quality bacon instead. Mashed sweet potato makes a colourful and delicious accompaniment to this dish — see our recipe on page 85.

1.3 kg (3 lb) pork loin rack,
  with 4 chops
75 g (2½ oz) piece of pancetta,
  about 1 cm (½ inch) thick, chopped
1 red onion, thinly sliced
1 green capsicum (pepper), trimmed,
  seeded and thinly sliced
1 green apple, peeled, cored and
  thinly sliced
2 garlic cloves, finely chopped
4 small rosemary sprigs, plus extra
  leaves, for sprinkling
250 ml (9 fl oz/1 cup) good-quality
  chicken stock
1 tablespoon cornflour (cornstarch)
125 ml (4 fl oz/½ cup) cream
400 g (14 oz) tin butterbeans
  (lima beans), rinsed and drained
400 g (14 oz) tin corn kernels,
  drained
2 tablespoons finely chopped flat-leaf
  (Italian) parsley

Trim the pork rack of skin and excess fat. Season generously with sea salt and freshly ground black pepper.

Place the pork rack in a slow cooker. Scatter the pancetta, onion, capsicum, apple, garlic and rosemary sprigs over, then pour in the stock.

Cover and cook on high for 4 hours, or until the pork and vegetables are tender.

Using tongs, remove the pork rack to a warmed plate. Cover with foil and leave to rest in a warm place while finishing the sauce.

Blend the cornflour with 1 tablespoon water until smooth. Stir the mixture into the sauce in the slow cooker, together with the cream. Cover and cook for 10 minutes to thicken the sauce a little.

Stir in the butterbeans, corn kernels and half the parsley, then cook for a further 5 minutes to warm the beans and corn.

To serve, carve the loin into 4 cutlets and divide among serving plates. Spoon the vegetables and sauce over. Sprinkle with the remaining parsley and extra rosemary and serve.

✳ **Preparation time:** 25 minutes ✳ **Cooking time:** 4 hours 15 minutes ✳ **Serves:** 4

Preparation time: 30 minutes
plus 30 minutes chilling

Cooking time: 8 hours 15 minutes

Serves: 4

Lamb meatballs with spicy saffron sauce

2 tablespoons olive oil
400 g (14 oz) fresh pappardelle
grated parmesan, to serve
basil leaves, to garnish

Meatballs

650 g (1 lb 7 oz) minced (ground) lamb
100 g (3½ oz/1 cup) dry breadcrumbs
1 egg, lightly beaten
1 garlic clove, crushed
2 teaspoons dried oregano
½ teaspoon sea salt
½ teaspoon freshly ground black pepper
2 tablespoons olive oil

Spicy saffron sauce

1 teaspoon saffron threads
115 g (4 oz/¾ cup) blanched almonds,
  toasted
1 garlic clove, crushed
55 g (2 oz/½ cup) ground hazelnuts
2 tablespoons tomato passata (puréed
  tomatoes)
2 tablespoons red wine vinegar
340 g (12 oz) jar roasted red capsicum
  (pepper) strips, drained
2 x 400 g (14 oz) tins chopped tomatoes
2 teaspoons paprika
1 teaspoon cayenne pepper
1 teaspoon chilli flakes
2 teaspoons soft brown sugar

To make the meatballs, combine the meatball ingredients in a large bowl and mix together well using your hands.

Using clean wet hands, form the mixture into 24 meatballs, using about one heaped tablespoon of mixture per ball. Place the meatballs on a plate, then cover and refrigerate for 30 minutes.

Meanwhile, make the spicy saffron sauce. In a small bowl, soak the saffron in 2 tablespoons hot water for 5 minutes to infuse.

Place the almonds and garlic in a food processor and pulse until a smooth paste forms. Add the ground hazelnuts, passata, vinegar, capsicum and one tin of chopped tomatoes and process to a smooth consistency. Add the saffron water, paprika, cayenne pepper, chilli flakes and sugar and pulse until thoroughly mixed. Pour the mixture into a slow cooker.

Heat the olive oil in a frying pan over medium heat. Add the meatballs in batches and fry for 3–4 minutes each time, or until evenly browned, turning often and transferring each batch to the slow cooker.

Cover and cook on low for 8 hours.

Meanwhile, near serving time, add the pasta to a large pot of rapidly boiling salted water and cook according to the packet instructions until al dente. Drain well.

Divide the pasta among serving bowls. Season the meatball mixture to taste with sea salt and freshly ground black pepper, then spoon the meatballs and sauce over the top. Sprinkle with parmesan and basil leaves and serve.

For a richer version of this dish, stir 185 ml (6 fl oz/¾ cup) cream through the finished meatball mixture just before serving it over the pasta.

Marmalade-glazed corned beef

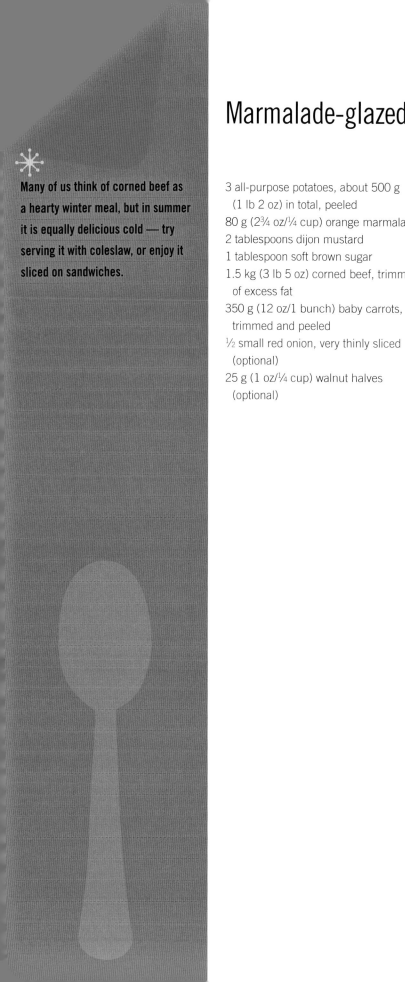

Many of us think of corned beef as a hearty winter meal, but in summer it is equally delicious cold — try serving it with coleslaw, or enjoy it sliced on sandwiches.

3 all-purpose potatoes, about 500 g (1 lb 2 oz) in total, peeled
80 g (2¾ oz/¼ cup) orange marmalade
2 tablespoons dijon mustard
1 tablespoon soft brown sugar
1.5 kg (3 lb 5 oz) corned beef, trimmed of excess fat
350 g (12 oz/1 bunch) baby carrots, trimmed and peeled
½ small red onion, very thinly sliced (optional)
25 g (1 oz/¼ cup) walnut halves (optional)

Cut the potatoes into large chunks and place them in a slow cooker.

In a small bowl, mix together 2 tablespoons of the marmalade, the mustard and sugar.

Rub the marmalade mixture all over the beef, rubbing it in well. Rest the corned beef in the slow cooker, on top of the potatoes, and drizzle with any marmalade mixture remaining in the bowl.

Cover and cook for 6 hours on low.

Add the carrots to the slow cooker, then cover and cook for another 2 hours.

Remove the corned beef from the slow cooker and place on a warmed platter. Cover with foil and set aside to rest in a warm place for 10 minutes before carving.

Meanwhile, melt the remaining marmalade. To do this, either warm it in the microwave in a microwave-safe bowl for about 20 seconds, or place it in a small saucepan over low heat and cook, stirring, for 1–2 minutes. Brush the marmalade over the hot beef to glaze it.

Carve the beef into thick slices. Serve with the potatoes and baby carrots, sprinkled with red onion slices and walnut halves if desired.

Preparation time: 15 minutes   **Cooking time:** 8 hours   **Serves:** 4–6

Preparation time: 20 minutes
plus 24 hours marinating

Cooking time: 6 hours 15 minutes

Serves: 4

Beef short ribs with molasses, bourbon and thyme

8 beef short ribs, about 2 kg (4 lb 8 oz)
  in total, separated
1 tablespoon olive oil
2 onions, chopped
2 carrots, peeled, cut in half lengthways
  and sliced
4 garlic cloves, chopped
125 ml (4 fl oz/½ cup) red wine
690 ml (24 fl oz) jar tomato passata
  (puréed tomatoes)
115 g (4 oz/⅓ cup) molasses
60 ml (2 fl oz/¼ cup) bourbon
1 tablespoon dijon mustard
3 thyme sprigs, plus extra, to garnish
1 bay leaf
1 teaspoon freshly ground black pepper

Molasses marinade

375 ml (13 fl oz/1½ cups) beer
60 ml (2 fl oz/¼ cup) molasses
5 thyme sprigs
1 teaspoon sea salt
1 teaspoon chilli flakes
1 teaspoon mustard powder
60 ml (2 fl oz/¼ cup) worcestershire
  sauce

Mixed tomato salad

1 tomato, cut into wedges
8 cherry tomatoes
8 yellow baby roma (plum) tomatoes,
  halved
1 teaspoon thyme
1 tablespoon olive oil
2 teaspoons white balsamic vinegar
1 garlic clove, finely chopped

Place the molasses marinade ingredients in a small bowl and whisk to combine.

Arrange the ribs in a 30 x 25 cm (12 x 10 inch) rectangular dish in one layer. Pour the marinade over the ribs and toss to coat. Cover and marinate in the refrigerator for 24 hours, turning the ribs over after 12 hours.

Drain the ribs from the marinade and discard the marinade.

Heat the olive oil in a large frying pan over medium–high heat. Add the ribs in batches and fry for 2–3 minutes on each side, or until browned on all sides, turning regularly.

Place the ribs in a slow cooker with the remaining ingredients. Cover and cook on low for 6 hours.

Meanwhile, near serving time, make the mixed tomato salad. Put all the tomatoes in a bowl and sprinkle with the thyme. Whisk together the olive oil, vinegar and garlic, then season to taste with sea salt and freshly ground black pepper. Drizzle the dressing over the tomatoes and gently mix together.

Skim any fat from the sauce in the slow cooker. Arrange the ribs on serving plates and drizzle generously with the sauce. Garnish with extra thyme and serve with the mixed tomato salad.

Cajun chicken stew

1.5 kg (3 lb 5 oz) chicken thigh fillets,
    trimmed of fat and cut in half
1 tablespoon cajun seasoning
2 tablespoons olive oil
375 ml (13 fl oz/1½ cups) good-quality
    chicken stock
400 g (14 oz) tin chopped tomatoes
1 green capsicum (pepper),
    trimmed, seeded and cut into
    1 cm (½ inch) pieces
2 celery stalks, thinly sliced
1 large onion, diced
60 ml (2 fl oz/¼ cup) worcestershire
    sauce
3 bay leaves
1 teaspoon sugar
1 garlic clove, crushed
1 teaspoon freshly ground black pepper
400 g (14 oz/2 cups) basmati rice

Put the chicken thighs in a large bowl. Sprinkle the cajun seasoning over them and toss until evenly coated.

Heat the olive oil in a large frying pan over medium heat. Add the chicken in batches and fry for 3–4 minutes, or until browned, turning occasionally and transferring each batch to a slow cooker.

Add all the remaining ingredients, except the rice, to the slow cooker. Mix together well.

Cover and cook on low for 6 hours.

Meanwhile, near serving time, prepare the rice. Rinse the rice under cold running water until the water runs clear. Place the rice and 375 ml (13 fl oz/1½ cups) cold water in a large saucepan, then cover and cook over low heat for 20–25 minutes, or until the rice is tender.

Spoon the rice onto serving plates or into wide shallow bowls. Ladle the chicken mixture over the top and serve.

✳ **Preparation time:** 15 minutes ✳ **Cooking time:** 6 hours 15 minutes ✳ **Serves:** 6

Preparation time: 20 minutes   **Cooking time:** 4 hours 20 minutes   **Serves:** 4–6

Cream of parsnip soup

1 kg (2 lb 4 oz) parsnips, peeled
and chopped
200 g (7 oz) all-purpose potatoes, such
as sebago, peeled and chopped
1 granny smith apple, peeled, cored
and chopped
1 onion, finely chopped
1 garlic clove, chopped
750 ml (26 fl oz/3 cups) good-quality
chicken stock
a pinch of saffron threads
250 ml (9 fl oz/1 cup) cream
snipped chives, to serve

Place the parsnip, potato, apple, onion, garlic, stock and saffron threads in a slow cooker.

Cover and cook on high for 4 hours.

Transfer the mixture to a food processor or blender, in batches if necessary. Purée to a soup consistency, then season to taste with sea salt.

Return the soup to the slow cooker and stir in the cream. Cover and cook for a further 20 minutes.

Ladle the soup into serving bowls. Serve sprinkled with chives and plenty of freshly ground black pepper.

For a vegetarian soup, replace the chicken stock with vegetable stock. For a sensational dinner party starter, serve this soup topped with pan-fried scallops.

Veal cacciatore

1½ tablespoons plain (all-purpose) flour
1 kg (2 lb 4 oz) veal osso buco (about 6 pieces)
1 onion, chopped
2 garlic cloves, crushed
1 red capsicum (pepper), trimmed, seeded and cut into 2 cm (¾ inch) chunks
1 bay leaf
2 anchovies, chopped
125 ml (4 fl oz/½ cup) good-quality chicken stock
400 g (14 oz) tin chopped tomatoes
1 tablespoon tomato paste (concentrated purée)
125 ml (4 fl oz/½ cup) white wine
90 g (3¼ oz/½ cup) pitted kalamata olives
400 g (14 oz/2 cups) risoni
30 g (1 oz) butter
small handful basil leaves, to serve

Put the flour in a bowl and season with sea salt and freshly ground black pepper. Toss the veal lightly in the seasoned flour.

Place the veal in a slow cooker and sprinkle with any remaining flour. Add the onion, garlic, capsicum and bay leaf.

In a small bowl, mash the anchovies to a paste using the back of a spoon. Blend with the stock and add to the slow cooker, along with the tomatoes, tomato paste and wine.

Cover and cook on high for 4 hours, or until the veal is tender.

Remove the lid and cook, uncovered, for a further 30 minutes to thicken the sauce a little. Season the sauce with sea salt and freshly ground black pepper. Stir in the olives.

Meanwhile, near serving time, add the risoni to a large pot of rapidly boiling salted water and cook according to the packet instructions until al dente. Drain well and stir the butter through.

Spoon the risoni into wide shallow serving bowls, then ladle the veal mixture over the top. Sprinkle with the basil and serve.

Preparation time: 20 minutes ✳ **Cooking time:** 4 hours 30 minutes ✳ **Serves:** 6

Preparation time: 15 minutes
plus overnight marinating (optional)

Cooking time: 8 hours

Serves: 4

Chinese braised lamb

60 ml (2 fl oz/¼ cup) hoisin sauce
2 teaspoons finely grated fresh ginger
2 garlic cloves, thinly sliced
2 star anise
1 tablespoon dark soy sauce
1 tablespoon dry sherry
1 tablespoon tomato sauce (ketchup)
1 teaspoon sesame oil
1 kg (2 lb 4 oz) lamb shoulder, boned
   and diced into 3–4 cm (1¼–1½ inch)
   pieces (ask your butcher to do this)
400 g (14 oz/2 cups) jasmine rice
6 spring onions (scallions), thinly sliced
   on the diagonal
steamed Asian greens, to serve

In a large bowl, mix together the hoisin sauce, ginger, garlic, star anise, soy sauce, sherry, tomato sauce and sesame oil. Add the lamb and toss until well coated. Cover and marinate in the refrigerator overnight if desired.

Transfer the lamb mixture to a slow cooker, adding all the marinade from the bowl.

Cover and cook on low for 8 hours, stirring occasionally.

Meanwhile, near serving time, prepare the rice. Rinse the rice under cold running water until the water runs clear. Place the rice in a saucepan with 450 ml (16 fl oz) water. Bring to the boil and boil for 1 minute. Cover tightly, reduce the heat to as low as possible and cook for 10 minutes. Remove from the heat and leave to stand, covered, for 10 minutes.

Spoon the rice onto serving plates or into wide shallow bowls, then ladle the lamb mixture over the top. Drizzle with the cooking juices, sprinkle with the spring onion and serve with steamed Asian greens.

Ask your butcher for the lamb bones from the shoulder and cook them in with the diced meat for a tastier sauce. Remove and discard before serving. If you can't find lamb shoulder, you can use lamb leg instead. If you're in a hurry you can cook the lamb on high, reducing the cooking time to 5–6 hours.

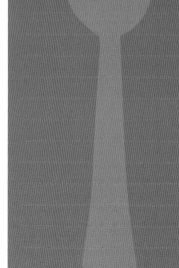

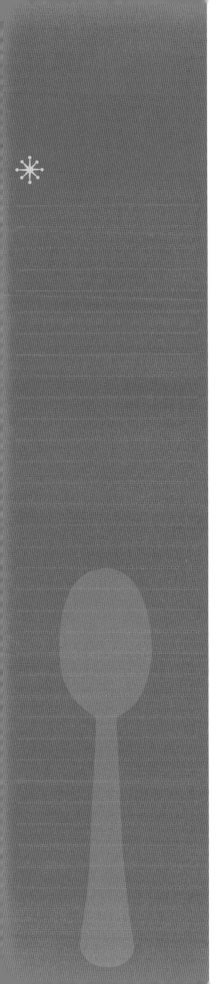

Braised teriyaki beef with udon noodles

olive oil, for brushing
1 small onion, chopped
375 ml (13 fl oz/1½ cups) teriyaki
   marinade
125 ml (4 fl oz/½ cup) good-quality
   beef stock
1 garlic clove, crushed
1.25 kg (2 lb 12 oz) budget rump steaks,
   cut into 4 cm (1½ inch) chunks
440 g (15½ oz) fresh udon noodles
3 spring onions (scallions), thinly sliced,
   plus extra, to garnish

Asian salad

1 small handful coriander (cilantro)
   leaves
1 red capsicum (pepper), trimmed,
   seeded and cut into matchsticks
1 large carrot, peeled and cut into
   matchsticks
1 Lebanese (short) cucumber,
   seeded and cut into matchsticks
2 tablespoons light soy sauce
1 tablespoon peanut oil
2 tablespoons lime juice
1 teaspoon white sesame seeds

Lightly brush the bowl of a slow cooker with olive oil. Add the onion to the slow cooker.

In a large bowl, mix together the teriyaki marinade, stock and garlic.

Add the beef to the marinade and toss until well coated. Thread the beef onto 12 small bamboo skewers and place the skewers in the slow cooker.

Cover and cook on low for 7½ hours, turning the skewers over at least once, if possible.

Place the noodles in a heatproof bowl and cover with boiling water. Allow to soak for a few minutes, until the noodles have softened.

Remove the skewers from the slow cooker. Drain the noodles and add to the slow cooker with the spring onion. Stir to coat the noodles with the sauce.

Place the skewers on top of the noodles, then cover and cook for another 30 minutes, or until the noodles are heated through.

Meanwhile, near serving time, make the Asian salad. Put the coriander, capsicum, carrot and cucumber in a bowl and toss to combine. Whisk together the soy sauce, peanut oil and lime juice, then pour over the salad. Toss gently and sprinkle with the sesame seeds.

Serve the skewers on a bed of noodles, sprinkled with extra spring onion. Serve the Asian salad on the side.

Preparation time: 25 minutes   **Cooking time:** 8 hours 40 minutes   **Serves:** 6

Bacon-wrapped pork cooked with maple syrup

1.25 kg (2 lb 12 oz) piece of pork neck, trimmed of any visible fat
6 rindless bacon slices, about 400 g (14 oz) in total
olive oil, for brushing
2 rosemary sprigs
125 ml (4 fl oz/½ cup) maple syrup
1 tablespoon cornflour (cornstarch)
steamed asparagus, to serve

Creamy celeriac and potato mash

1 celeriac
1 large roasting potato, such as russet or king idaho, peeled and cut into 2.5 cm (1 inch) chunks
250 ml (9 fl oz/1 cup) milk
20 g (¾ oz) unsalted butter, softened

Season the pork with sea salt and freshly ground black pepper.

Cut six lengths of kitchen string, each about 80 cm (31½ inches) long. Lay them on a clean work surface, evenly spaced to the width of the pork. Lay the bacon slices so they just overlap on top of the string, and run the same way as the string. Place the pork in the centre of the bacon. Roll up firmly and tie the strings to secure the pork into a roll — the bacon should cover the top of the pork.

Heat a large non-stick frying pan over high heat. Add the pork and brown for 10 minutes, turning regularly.

Lightly brush the bowl of a slow cooker with olive oil. Place the rosemary sprigs in the slow cooker and rest the pork on top. Season again with freshly ground black pepper, then pour the maple syrup over.

Cover and cook on low heat for 8 hours, or until the pork is very tender. Transfer the pork to a warm platter and cover with foil. Leave to rest in a warm place while finishing the sauce.

Turn the slow cooker setting to high. Blend the cornflour with 1 tablespoon water until smooth, then stir into the sauce. Cover and cook for a further 30 minutes, or until the sauce is slightly thickened.

Meanwhile, make the celeriac and potato mash. Trim and peel the celeriac, then chop into 2.5 cm (1 inch) chunks. Place in a saucepan with the potato and milk and bring to the boil over high heat. Cover and cook for 15 minutes, or until tender. Mash well and season to taste with sea salt and freshly ground black pepper. Stir in the butter and keep warm.

Carve the pork into thick slices and drizzle with the sauce from the slow cooker. Serve with the celeriac and potato mash and steamed asparagus.

Greek lamb with risoni and feta

Risoni, also known as orzo, is a small rice-shaped pasta. You'll find it in continental delicatessens and larger supermarkets. If unavailable, use macaroni here instead.

1 kg (2 lb 4 oz) diced lamb
2 small red onions, finely chopped
2 garlic cloves, crushed
2 bay leaves
2 x 400 g (14 oz) tins chopped tomatoes
125 ml (4 fl oz/½ cup) good-quality
   chicken stock
125 ml (4 fl oz/½ cup) white wine
220 g (7½ oz/1 cup) risoni
75 g (2½ oz/½ cup) crumbled feta
   cheese
1 tablespoon grated lemon rind
2 tablespoons small oregano leaves
crusty bread, to serve

Greek salad
1 Lebanese (short) cucumber
4 vine-ripened tomatoes, cut into
   wedges
10 kalamata olives
200 g (7 oz/1⅓ cups) crumbled
   Greek feta cheese
60 ml (2 fl oz/¼ cup) extra virgin olive oil
1 tablespoon lemon juice

Put the lamb, onion, garlic, bay leaves and tomatoes in a slow cooker. Pour in the stock and wine and mix together.

Cover and cook on low for 7 hours, or until the lamb is very tender.

Sprinkle the risoni over the lamb and mix it in well. Cover and cook for a further 40 minutes, or until the risoni is tender.

Meanwhile, near serving time, make the Greek salad. Cut the cucumber in half lengthways, discard the seeds, then cut into bite-sized pieces. Place in a serving bowl with the tomato, olives and feta. Whisk together the olive oil and lemon juice, pour over the salad and gently toss together.

Season the lamb mixture generously with freshly ground black pepper.

Divide the lamb mixture among wide shallow serving bowls, then sprinkle with the feta, lemon rind and oregano. Serve with the Greek salad and crusty bread.

※ **Preparation time:** 15 minutes ※ **Cooking time:** 7 hours 40 minutes ※ **Serves:** 4–6

Preparation time: 15 minutes ✳ **Cooking time:** 3 hours 15 minutes ✳ **Serves:** 4

Spanish chicken

6 skinless chicken thigh fillets,
  about 750 g (1 lb 10 oz) in total
2 chorizo sausages, chopped
1 red onion, chopped
100 g (3½ oz) roasted red
  capsicum (pepper) pieces
  (from a jar), thinly sliced
4 garlic cloves, finely chopped
1 green chilli, seeded and finely
  chopped
2 teaspoons smoked paprika
1 teaspoon dried oregano
400 g (14 oz) tin chopped tomatoes
375 ml (13 fl oz/1½ cups) good-quality
  chicken stock
155 g (5½ oz/1 cup) fresh or frozen peas
crusty bread, to serve

Trim the chicken thighs of excess fat, then
cut into 3 cm (1¼ inch) chunks.

Place the chicken in a slow cooker with
the chorizo, onion, capsicum, garlic, chilli,
paprika, oregano, tomatoes and stock. Season
with sea salt and freshly ground black pepper
and mix together well.

Cover and cook on high for 3 hours.

Stir the peas through and cook for a
further 15 minutes, or until the peas are
warmed through.

Ladle into serving bowls and serve with
crusty bread.

A signature spice in Spanish cuisine,
smoked paprika is made from
capsicums (peppers) that have been
slowly smoked, then ground to a fine
powder. It is widely available, but
if you don't have any, you can use
sweet paprika here.

Savoury mince

Any leftover savoury mince can be made into turnovers. Cut some circles from some thawed sheets of frozen puff pastry. Place some savoury mince on one half of each circle, then fold the pastry over to enclose. Place the turnovers on a baking tray and bake in a preheated 200°C (400°F/Gas 6) oven for 20 minutes, or until the pastry is puffed and golden.

1 kg (2 lb 4 oz) lean minced (ground) beef
2 garlic cloves, crushed
250 g (9 oz/¾ cup) fruit chutney
500 ml (17 fl oz/2 cups) good-quality beef stock
3 potatoes, about 800 g (1 lb 12 oz) in total, peeled and chopped
2 carrots, peeled and chopped
2 rosemary sprigs
155 g (5½ oz/1 cup) fresh or frozen peas
4 tablespoons roughly chopped flat-leaf (Italian) parsley
hot buttered toast, to serve

Place the beef, garlic, chutney, stock, potato, carrot and rosemary in a slow cooker. Mix together well.

Cover and cook on low for 6 hours.

Stir the peas through, then cover and cook for a further 15 minutes, or until the peas are warmed through.

Season to taste with sea salt and freshly ground black pepper. Stir the parsley through and serve with hot buttered toast.

Preparation time: 10 minutes **Cooking time:** 6 hours 15 minutes **Serves:** 6

Preparation time: 25 minutes ✳ **Cooking time:** 7 hours 10 minutes ✳ **Serves:** 6

Abruzzi-style lamb

2 red capsicums (peppers)
400 g (14 oz) tin chopped tomatoes
1.5 kg (3 lb 5 oz) leg of lamb, trimmed
  of any visible fat
2 onions, thinly sliced
2 garlic cloves, finely chopped
1 tablespoon tomato paste
  (concentrated purée)
a pinch of sugar
2 small rosemary sprigs
3 oregano sprigs
125 ml (4 fl oz/½ cup) white wine
125 ml (4 fl oz/½ cup) good-quality
  chicken stock
2 tablespoons roughly chopped flat-leaf
  (Italian) parsley
thyme sprigs, to garnish
cooked cannellini beans, to serve
steamed asparagus, to serve

Preheat the grill (broiler) to high.

Cut the capsicums into quarters and remove the seeds and membranes. Place them on the grill tray, skin side up. Grill (broil) for 5–10 minutes, or until the skins have blistered and blackened. Place the capsicum in a bowl, cover and allow to cool. Peel off the skin and cut the flesh into thin strips. Set aside.

In a blender or food processor, purée the tomatoes until smooth.

Place the lamb in a slow cooker. Add the capsicum, puréed tomatoes, onion, garlic, tomato paste, sugar, rosemary and oregano sprigs. In a cup or small bowl, mix together the wine and stock. Pour over the lamb and stir together gently.

Cover and cook on low for 3½ hours.

Carefully turn the lamb over, then cover and cook for a further 3½ hours — the lamb should be falling off the bone.

Carefully remove the lamb from the slow cooker and place on a chopping board. Carve into thick slices.

Season the sauce in the slow cooker with sea salt and freshly ground black pepper to taste.

Serve the lamb drizzled with the sauce and garnished with thyme sprigs, with cannellini beans and steamed asparagus on the side.

If the sauce is too thin for your liking, transfer it to a saucepan and simmer over medium heat for 15 minutes, or until thickened. This recipe is also delicious served with soft polenta — see our recipe on page 157.

Spicy

Vietnamese caramel chicken • Pork and lemongrass curry • Indian-style vegetable curry • Pulled pork • Vietnamese chicken curry • Indonesian beef stew • Curried cauliflower and red lentil soup • Red cooked chicken • Jamaican lamb with sweet potato mash • Spiced carrot soup with coriander pesto • Mojo pork • Tamarind lamb • Tunisian chickpea and silverbeet soup • Egyptian beef with okra • Lamb shanks braised with quince paste • Green curry of tofu and vegetables • Lebanese lamb stew • Moroccan fish tagine • African chicken • Thai chilli basil pork ribs • Five-spice caramel pork • Thai-style pumpkin soup • Moroccan ratatouille • Chicken tikka masala • Vegetarian chilli beans • Chinese-style beef with cumin • Salmon tom kha • Yoghurt-marinated lamb with garlic and spices • Curried chicken and peanut soup • Prawn laksa lemak • Vietnamese beef brisket • Chicken and lentil curry • Sri Lankan fish curry • Chilli and anchovy lamb neck • Chicken with harissa

Preparation time: 10 minutes **Cooking time:** 5 hours 10 minutes **Serves:** 4–6

Vietnamese caramel chicken

1 kg (2 lb 4 oz) skinless, bone-in chicken
  thighs, flesh scored
2 lemongrass stems, bruised
400 g (14 oz/2 cups) jasmine rice
2 small carrots, peeled and cut into
  thin slivers, to garnish
3 spring onions (scallions), sliced on
  the diagonal
roasted peanuts, to garnish
baby basil leaves, to garnish

Caramel sauce
1 tablespoon peanut oil
2 teaspoons grated fresh ginger
2 garlic cloves, crushed
80 ml (2½ fl oz/⅓ cup) soy sauce
125 g (4½ oz/⅔ cup) dark brown sugar
60 ml (2 fl oz/¼ cup) fish sauce
60 ml (2 fl oz/¼ cup) Chinese rice wine

To make the caramel sauce, heat the peanut oil in a small saucepan over medium heat; add the ginger and garlic and cook for 1 minute. Add the soy sauce and sugar and cook, stirring, for 3 minutes until the sugar has dissolved. Add the fish sauce and rice wine and reduce the heat to low. Simmer for 5 minutes, or until the sauce has thickened to a syrup consistency.

Place the chicken in a slow cooker and pour the caramel sauce over the chicken. Turn to coat the chicken with the sauce. Add the lemongrass.

Cover and cook on low for 5 hours, or until the chicken is tender.

Meanwhile, near serving time, prepare the rice. Rinse the rice under cold running water until the water runs clear. Place the rice in a saucepan with 450 ml (16 fl oz) water. Bring to the boil and boil for 1 minute. Cover tightly, reduce the heat to as low as possible and cook for 10 minutes. Remove from the heat and leave to stand, covered, for 10 minutes.

Spoon the rice into wide shallow bowls, then ladle the chicken mixture over the top. Garnish with the carrot, spring onion, peanuts and basil leaves and serve.

Bruising the lemongrass stems helps to release the flavours. To do this, hit the stems with the back of a cleaver or heavy knife. If you're in a hurry you can cook the chicken on high, reducing the cooking time to 3½ hours.

Pork and lemongrass curry

1 tablespoon peanut oil
1 kg (2 lb 4 oz) pork shoulder, cut into
  2 cm (¾ inch) chunks
270 ml (9½ fl oz) tin coconut cream
400 g (14 oz/2 cups) jasmine rice
40 g (1½ oz/¼ cup) roasted peanuts,
  chopped, to garnish
1 small handful chopped mint, to garnish
1 long red chilli, thinly sliced, to garnish
lime wedges, to serve

Lemongrass curry paste
1 onion, chopped
2 garlic cloves, chopped
2 small bird's eye chillies, chopped
2 red Asian shallots, peeled and chopped
3 tablespoons chopped lemongrass,
  white part only
1 handful coriander (cilantro) leaves,
  chopped
2 tablespoons Thai green curry paste

To make the lemongrass curry paste, place the onion, garlic, chilli, shallots, lemongrass, coriander, curry paste and 2 tablespoons water in a food processor and process to form a smooth paste. Set aside.

Heat the peanut oil in a large frying pan over medium heat. Add the pork in batches and fry for 5 minutes, turning to brown all over and transferring each batch to a slow cooker.

Add any pan juices from the pork to the slow cooker. Stir in the lemongrass curry paste, then pour in the coconut cream.

Cover and cook on low for 6 hours.

Meanwhile, near serving time, prepare the rice. Rinse the rice under cold running water until the water runs clear. Place the rice in a saucepan with 450 ml (16 fl oz) water. Bring to the boil and boil for 1 minute. Cover tightly, reduce the heat to as low as possible and cook for 10 minutes. Remove from the heat and leave to stand, covered, for 10 minutes.

Spoon the rice into wide shallow bowls, then ladle the pork mixture over the top. Sprinkle with the peanuts, mint and chilli and serve with lime wedges.

Preparation time: 15 minutes **Cooking time:** 6 hours 20 minutes **Serves:** 4

✳ **Preparation time:** 15 minutes ✳ **Cooking time:** 6 hours 30 minutes ✳ **Serves:** 4

Indian-style vegetable curry

1 onion, finely chopped
2 teaspoons finely grated fresh ginger
55 g (2 oz/¼ cup) mild curry paste
  (such as balti)
1 small handful curry leaves
375 ml (13 fl oz/1½ cups) good-quality
  vegetable stock
350 g (12 oz/2¾ cups) cauliflower florets
300 g (10½ oz) sweet potato, peeled
  and cut into 2 cm (¾ inch) chunks
1 zucchini (courgette), sliced
2 ripe tomatoes, chopped
60 g (2¼ oz/¼ cup) plain yoghurt
400 g (14 oz) tin brown lentils, rinsed
  and drained
45 g (1½ oz/1 cup) baby English
  spinach leaves
155 g (5½ oz/1 cup) frozen peas,
  thawed
3 tablespoons chopped coriander
  (cilantro) leaves
400 g (14 oz/2 cups) basmati rice

Put the onion, ginger, curry paste, curry leaves and stock in a slow cooker. Add the cauliflower, sweet potato, zucchini and tomato and gently mix together.

Cover and cook on low for 6 hours, or until the vegetables are tender.

Stir in the yoghurt, lentils, spinach, peas and half the coriander. Cover and cook on high for a further 30 minutes, or until the spinach has wilted.

Meanwhile, prepare the rice. Rinse the rice under cold running water until the water runs clear. Place the rice and 375 ml (13 fl oz/ 1½ cups) cold water in a large saucepan, then cover and cook over low heat for 20–25 minutes, or until the rice is tender.

Spoon the rice into wide shallow bowls, then ladle the curry over the top. Sprinkle with the remaining coriander and serve.

Curry leaves are highly aromatic and used extensively in Sri Lankan and southern Indian cooking, particularly in curries. They are available in Asian food stores and in larger supermarkets.

Pulled pork

3 kg (6 lb 12 oz) piece of pork leg roast
1 large onion, very finely chopped
125 ml (4 fl oz/½ cup) tomato sauce
  (ketchup)
80 ml (2½ fl oz/⅓ cup) cider vinegar
55 g (2 oz/¼ cup) soft brown sugar
1½ tablespoons molasses
2 tablespoons tomato paste
  (concentrated purée)
2 tablespoons dijon mustard
1 tablespoon sweet paprika
1 teaspoon cayenne pepper
2 teaspoons cumin seeds
2 dried bay leaves
2½ teaspoons dried oregano
2½ tablespoons plain (all-purpose) flour
toasted bread slices, to serve
sliced gherkins (pickles), to serve

Coleslaw
60 g (2¼ oz/¼ cup) whole-egg
  mayonnaise
2 tablespoons lemon juice
125 g (4½ oz/1⅔ cups) finely shredded
  green cabbage
2 small carrots, peeled and roughly
  grated

Remove the skin and the layer of fat from the pork roast, then place the pork in a slow cooker.

In a bowl, combine the onion, tomato sauce, vinegar, sugar, molasses, tomato paste, mustard, paprika, cayenne pepper and cumin seeds. Stir until smooth, then pour over the pork in the slow cooker. Add the bay leaves.

Cover and cook on low for 8 hours, or until the pork is very tender.

Remove the pork to a large plate or bowl and leave to cool slightly.

Add the oregano to the slow cooker and turn the heat to high. In a small bowl, combine the flour with 250 ml (9 fl oz/1 cup) of the cooking liquid, whisking until smooth. Whisk the flour mixture into the liquid in the slow cooker. Cover and cook for 30–35 minutes, or until the sauce has thickened, whisking occasionally to prevent lumps forming.

Meanwhile, make the coleslaw. Combine the mayonnaise and lemon juice in a large bowl and mix well. Add the cabbage and carrot and toss until well combined. Set aside.

Shred the pork, using your hands. Add the shredded pork to the slow cooker, then cover and cook on high for a final 10 minutes, or until the pork is heated through.

Serve the pulled pork on toasted bread, with the coleslaw and gherkins.

Preparation time: 20 minutes   **Cooking time:** 8 hours 45 minutes   **Serves:** 6–8

☀ **Preparation time:** 15 minutes   ☀ **Cooking time:** 6 hours   ☀ **Serves:** 6

Vietnamese chicken curry

1 kg (2 lb 4 oz) skinless chicken thigh
  fillets, trimmed and quartered
1 sweet potato, peeled and cut into
  2.5 cm (1 inch) chunks
1 tablespoon mild Indian curry powder
1 tablespoon caster (superfine) sugar
1 lemongrass stem, bruised
3 bay leaves
400 ml (14 fl oz) tin coconut milk
250 ml (9 fl oz/1 cup) good-quality
  chicken stock
400 g (14 oz/2 cups) jasmine rice
2 teaspoons fish sauce
lime wedges, to serve

Cucumber and tomato salad
1 Lebanese (short) cucumber,
  seeded and sliced
12 cherry tomatoes, quartered
1 red chilli, thinly sliced
25 g (1 oz/¼ cup) bean sprouts,
  tails trimmed
1 small handful coriander (cilantro)
  leaves
1 teaspoon lime juice
¼ teaspoon sesame oil

Put the chicken and sweet potato in a slow cooker. Sprinkle with the curry powder and sugar and gently mix them through. Add the lemongrass and bay leaves, then pour in the coconut milk and stock.

Cover and cook on low for 6 hours.

Meanwhile, near serving time, prepare the rice. Rinse the rice under cold running water until the water runs clear. Place the rice in a saucepan with 450 ml (16 fl oz) water. Bring to the boil and boil for 1 minute. Cover tightly, reduce the heat to as low as possible and cook for 10 minutes. Remove from the heat and leave to stand, covered, for 10 minutes.

Meanwhile, make the cucumber and tomato salad. Combine all the ingredients in a bowl and toss to combine.

Stir the fish sauce through the curry. Season to taste with freshly ground black pepper.

Spoon the rice into wide shallow bowls, then ladle the curry over the top. Serve with lime wedges and the cucumber and tomato salad.

For a hotter curry, add ½ teaspoon chilli powder and some chopped red chilli to the curry. Serve garnished with extra sliced chilli.

Indonesian beef stew

Kecap manis is a thick, sweet soy sauce originating from Indonesia. It is available from supermarkets and Asian grocery stores.

1 kg (2 lb 4 oz) topside or rump beef steak
1 onion, chopped
2 carrots, peeled and coarsely grated
2 garlic cloves, finely chopped
375 ml (13 fl oz/1½ cups) good-quality beef stock
1 teaspoon sesame oil
2 tablespoons kecap manis
1 tablespoon light soy sauce
1 tablespoon tomato sauce (ketchup)
1 tablespoon sweet chilli sauce
400 g (14 oz/2 cups) basmati rice
fried Asian shallots, to serve
1 small handful coriander (cilantro) leaves, to garnish

Trim the beef of excess fat, then cut into 4 cm (1½ inch) pieces. Place in a slow cooker.

In a bowl, mix together the onion, carrot, garlic, stock, sesame oil, kecap manis, soy sauce, tomato sauce and sweet chilli sauce. Pour over the beef and mix together well.

Cover and cook on high for 4 hours, or until the beef is tender.

Meanwhile, near serving time, prepare the rice. Rinse the rice under cold running water until the water runs clear. Place the rice and 375 ml (13 fl oz/1½ cups) cold water in a large saucepan, then cover and cook over low heat for 20–25 minutes, or until the rice is tender.

Ladle the stew into wide shallow serving bowls. Sprinkle with fried Asian shallots and coriander and serve with the rice.

Preparation time: 20 minutes   **Cooking time:** 4 hours   **Serves:** 6

Preparation time: 15 minutes ✳ **Cooking time:** 3 hours ✳ **Serves:** 6–8

Curried cauliflower and red lentil soup

1 kg (2 lb 4 oz) cauliflower
1 large onion
2 celery stalks
100 g (3½ oz/½ cup) red lentils
1½ tablespoons mild curry paste
400 ml (14 fl oz) tin coconut milk
1 litre (35 fl oz/4 cups) good-quality
  vegetable stock
2 tablespoons finely shredded mint
lime wedges, to serve

Cut the cauliflower, onion and celery into 2 cm (¾ inch) chunks. Place in a slow cooker with the lentils. In a small bowl, mix the curry paste with the coconut milk until smooth. Pour into the slow cooker, then pour in the stock.

Cover and cook on high for 3 hours, or until the vegetables are tender.

Remove and reserve a large ladleful of the cooked cauliflower. In a blender or food processor, blend the remaining soup in several batches until smooth. Season to taste with sea salt and freshly ground black pepper.

Ladle the soup into serving bowls. Top with the reserved cauliflower florets and the mint and serve with lime wedges.

This soup is delicious served with warmed naan bread, with some chopped cooked chicken stirred through. You could also serve it with a dollop of minted yoghurt, made by mixing 2 tablespoons finely chopped mint through 200 g (7 oz) yoghurt.

Red cooked chicken

2 x 1.2 kg (2 lb 10 oz) chickens,
  jointed
4 cm (1½ inch) piece of fresh ginger,
  peeled and sliced
115 g (4 oz/½ cup) soft brown sugar
1½ teaspoons fennel seeds
125 ml (4 fl oz/½ cup) hoisin sauce
250 ml (9 fl oz/1 cup) Chinese rice
  wine or medium–sweet sherry
250 ml (9 fl oz/1 cup) soy sauce
1 cinnamon stick
2 star anise
3 orange peel strips, each about
  2 cm (¾ inch) wide, white pith
  removed, plus thin orange rind
  strips, to garnish
500 ml (17 fl oz/2 cups) good-quality
  chicken stock
400 g (14 oz/2 cups) jasmine rice
2 spring onions (scallions), cut into
  long thin slivers
steamed bok choy (pak choy),
  to serve

Put the chicken pieces in a slow cooker. In a small bowl, combine the ginger, sugar, fennel seeds, hoisin sauce, rice wine and soy sauce. Mix well to dissolve the sugar, then pour over the chicken pieces. Add the cinnamon stick, star anise and thick orange peel strips, then pour in the stock.

Cover and cook on low for 5–6 hours.

Meanwhile, near serving time, prepare the rice. Rinse the rice under cold running water until the water runs clear. Place the rice in a saucepan with 450 ml (16 fl oz) water. Bring to the boil and boil for 1 minute. Cover tightly, reduce the heat to as low as possible and cook for 10 minutes. Remove from the heat and leave to stand, covered, for 10 minutes.

Remove the chicken from the slow cooker to a warmed platter, cover with foil and keep warm. Skim as much excess fat from the surface of the cooking liquid as possible. Discard the cinnamon stick, star anise and thick orange peel strips.

Divide the chicken among wide shallow serving bowls, then ladle the broth over the top. Garnish with orange zest strips and spring onion slivers. Serve with the rice and steamed bok choy.

Preparation time: 20 minutes   **Cooking time:** 6 hours   **Serves:** 6–8

Preparation time: 20 minutes　　**Cooking time:** 6 hours　　**Serves:** 4

Jamaican lamb with sweet potato mash

finely grated rind of 1 lime
60 ml (2 fl oz/¼ cup) lime juice
60 ml (2 fl oz/¼ cup) olive oil
3 garlic cloves, crushed
2 teaspoons ground cumin
1½ teaspoons cayenne pepper,
  or to taste
1 teaspoon ground allspice
1 teaspoon ground white pepper
1 teaspoon ground cinnamon
1 tablespoon thyme
1 kg (2 lb 4 oz) boneless, skinless
  lamb shoulder, cut into 4 cm
  (1½ inch) chunks
lime cheeks, to serve

Sweet potato mash
900 g (2 lb) sweet potato, peeled and
  cut into 3 cm (1¼ inch) chunks
1 teaspoon ground cinnamon
40 g (1½ oz) butter

Mango and red chilli salsa
1 mango, finely diced
2 spring onions (scallions), finely
  chopped
1 small red chilli, finely chopped

Put the lime rind, lime juice, olive oil, garlic, ground spices and thyme in a slow cooker. Add the lamb and gently mix until coated.

Cover and cook on low for 5–6 hours, or until the lamb is tender, fragrant and has a little browning on top.

Meanwhile, near serving time, make the sweet potato mash. Bring a saucepan of water to the boil, place the sweet potato in a steamer basket and set it over the saucepan. Steam the sweet potato for 10–15 minutes, or until tender. Place in a bowl, mash using a potato masher, then stir the cinnamon and butter through.

Put all the mango and red chilli salsa ingredients in a small bowl and gently mix together. Set aside.

Spoon the sweet potato mash into wide shallow serving bowls. Ladle the lamb mixture over the top. Serve with the mango and red chilli salsa, with lime cheeks for squeezing over.

To get the most juice from limes or other citrus fruit, heat them in a microwave for 20 seconds before juicing. If you're in a hurry you can cook the lamb on high, reducing the cooking time to 3½ hours. You can serve the finished dish drizzled with a little coconut milk if you wish.

Spiced carrot soup with coriander pesto

2 tablespoons olive oil
1 red onion, diced
1 garlic clove, finely chopped
1 teaspoon cumin seeds
1 teaspoon paprika
1 teaspoon garam masala
3 small red chillies, seeded and finely chopped
6 large carrots, peeled and chopped
1 kg (2 lb 4 oz) sweet potatoes, peeled and diced
2 large desiree potatoes, peeled and diced
1.5 litres (52 fl oz/6 cups) good-quality chicken stock
300 ml (10½ fl oz) coconut cream
toasted naan bread, to serve

Coriander pesto
45 g (1½ oz/¼ cup) cashew nuts
1 large handful coriander (cilantro) leaves
1 small garlic clove, halved
60 ml (2 fl oz/¼ cup) coconut milk
60 ml (2 fl oz/¼ cup) olive oil

Heat the olive oil in a frying pan over medium–high heat. Add the onion and garlic and cook, stirring often, for 2–3 minutes, or until the onion has softened. Stir in the spices and chilli and cook for a further 1 minute, or until aromatic.

Spoon the onion and garlic mixture into a slow cooker and add the chopped vegetables and stock. Mix together well.

Cover and cook on low for 8 hours.

Meanwhile, near serving time, make the coriander pesto. Place the cashews, coriander, garlic and coconut milk in a food processor and process until the nuts are finely chopped. With the motor running, gradually add the olive oil in a thin steady stream until well combined.

Using a stick blender, purée the soup until smooth. Stir the coconut cream through, then season to taste with sea salt and freshly ground black pepper.

Ladle the soup into serving bowls. Swirl some of the pesto over the top and serve with toasted naan bread.

Preparation time: 20 minutes ✳ **Cooking time:** 8 hours 5 minutes ✳ **Serves:** 6

Preparation time: 15 minutes   **Cooking time:** 8 hours   **Serves:** 6

Mojo pork

1.5 kg (3 lb 5 oz) boneless pork loin,
  cut into 2 cm (¾ inch) chunks
2 teaspoons dried oregano
1 teaspoon chilli flakes
½ teaspoon freshly ground black pepper
2 tablespoons olive oil
1 large red onion, finely sliced
2 x 400 g (14 oz) tins chopped tomatoes
60 ml (2 fl oz/¼ cup) lime juice
60 ml (2 fl oz/¼ cup) orange juice
250 ml (9 fl oz/1 cup) good-quality
  chicken stock
1 small handful coriander (cilantro)
  leaves, to garnish

Bean and orange salad

2 oranges, peel and white pith removed,
  cut into segments
300 g (10½ oz) tin butterbeans
  (lima beans), rinsed and drained
300 g (10½ oz) tin chickpeas, rinsed
  and drained
1 red onion, halved and finely sliced
1 small handful coriander (cilantro)
  leaves
2 tablespoons olive oil
2 tablespoons red wine vinegar
a pinch of caster (superfine) sugar

Remove the rind and fat from the pork loin,
then cut the meat into 2 cm (¾ inch) chunks.
Place the pork in a slow cooker and sprinkle
with the oregano, chilli flakes and pepper.
Drizzle with the olive oil and gently mix to
coat. Add the onion and tomatoes, then pour
in the lime juice, orange juice and stock.

Cover and cook on low for 6–8 hours, or
until the pork is tender.

Meanwhile, just before serving, make the
bean and orange salad. In a salad bowl, toss
together the orange segments, beans, chickpeas,
onion and coriander. Whisk together the olive
oil, vinegar and sugar until the sugar has
dissolved. Season to taste with sea salt and
freshly ground black pepper, drizzle over the
salad and gently toss.

Ladle the pork mixture onto serving plates.
Sprinkle with the coriander and serve with the
bean and orange salad.

'Mojo' ... ...uce that contains
spices and citrus juice (generally
lime and/or orange juice). It is used
in Cuban cooking.

Tamarind lamb

60 ml (2 fl oz/¼ cup) tamarind pulp
2 garlic cloves, crushed
1 tablespoon garam masala
1 teaspoon chilli flakes
1 teaspoon shrimp paste
1 teaspoon sugar
1 teaspoon freshly ground black pepper
½ teaspoon ground turmeric
2 tablespoons vegetable oil
1 kg (2 lb 4 oz) lamb shoulder, cut into
  2 cm (¾ inch) chunks
2 large onions, roughly chopped
500 ml (17 fl oz/2 cups) good-quality
  chicken stock
coriander (cilantro) sprigs, to garnish
lime wedges, to serve

Lemon couscous
375 ml (13 fl oz/1½ cups) good-quality
  chicken stock
280 g (10 oz/1½ cups) instant
  couscous
40 g (1½ oz) butter
1 teaspoon finely grated lemon rind
1½ tablespoons lemon juice

Put the tamarind pulp in a small bowl. Pour in 125 ml (4 fl oz/½ cup) hot water and mix well. Leave to soak for 5 minutes, then strain the mixture through a fine sieve into another small bowl, pressing on the solids with a spoon to extract all the pulp. Discard the solids.

Stir the garlic, garam masala, chilli flakes, shrimp paste, sugar, pepper and turmeric into the tamarind water and set aside.

Heat the oil in a frying pan over medium–high heat. Add the lamb in batches and fry for 2–3 minutes, or until brown on all sides. Transfer each batch to a slow cooker.

Scatter the onion over the lamb, then pour in the tamarind water and stock.

Cover and cook on low for 8 hours.

Meanwhile, near serving time, prepare the lemon couscous. Bring the stock to the boil in a saucepan. Remove from the heat, add the butter and stir until melted. Place the couscous in a heatproof bowl with the lemon rind and lemon juice. Season well with sea salt and freshly ground black pepper and pour the stock over. Cover with a tea towel (dish towel) and leave to stand for 5 minutes, or until the liquid is absorbed. Fluff the grains up with a fork.

Spoon the lamb mixture into wide shallow serving bowls. Garnish with coriander sprigs and serve with the couscous and lime wedges.

Preparation time: 20 minutes ✳ **Cooking time:** 8 hours 15 minutes ✳ **Serves:** 4

✳ **Preparation time:** 15 minutes ✳ **Cooking time:** 3 hours 40 minutes ✳ **Serves:** 4

Tunisian chickpea and silverbeet soup

1 tablespoon olive oil
1 onion, finely sliced
1 teaspoon ground white pepper
1 teaspoon freshly grated nutmeg
½ teaspoon ground cumin
¼ teaspoon ground cloves
¼ teaspoon ground cinnamon
2 x 400 g (14 oz) tins chickpeas,
    rinsed and drained
1 bunch silverbeet (Swiss chard),
    about 900 g (2 lb)
625 ml (21½ fl oz/2½ cups)
    good-quality chicken or vegetable
    stock
Greek yoghurt, to serve
crusty bread, to serve
lemon wedges, to serve

Heat the olive oil in a frying pan over medium–high heat. Add the onion and cook for 3 minutes, or until it starts to brown, stirring occasionally. Reduce the heat to low and cook for another 5 minutes, or until the onion is soft.

Add the white pepper, nutmeg, cumin, cloves and cinnamon and continue to cook, stirring, for another 30 seconds. Add the chickpeas and stir until they are well coated in the spiced onion. Transfer the mixture to a slow cooker.

Wash the silverbeet leaves well and shake dry. Remove the stem below the leaf and discard. Slice across the leaves and stems, cutting the silverbeet into 2 cm (¾ inch) ribbons.

Add the silverbeet to the slow cooker and pour in the stock. Gently mix together.

Cover and cook on low for 2½–3½ hours, or until the silverbeet is just tender.

Using a stick blender, process the soup in a few short bursts, just to blend a portion of the soup, but not to make it smooth — most of the chickpeas should still be whole. Season to taste with sea salt and freshly ground black pepper.

Ladle the soup into serving bowls and top with a small dollop of yoghurt. Serve with crusty bread and lemon wedges.

If you're in a hurry you can cook the soup on high, reducing the cooking time to 1½–2 hours. Once the soup has been cooked, the flavours will continue to improve if the soup is left to rest for 30 minutes or more.

Egyptian beef with okra

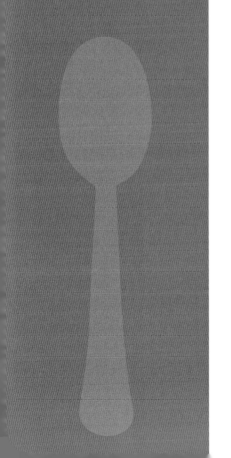

Filled with sticky seeds, okra is a small pod vegetable with a ridged, oblong shape. It is also known as 'lady fingers' or bamia. When slowly cooked, okra releases a viscous gum that acts as a thickener in stews and other dishes. It is best known as an ingredient in Louisiana gumbo.

2 tablespoons plain (all-purpose) flour
1 tablespoon ground cumin
2 teaspoons ground coriander
800 g (1 lb 12 oz) beef chuck steak, cut into 3 cm (1¼ inch) chunks
2 onions, chopped
3 garlic cloves, crushed
70 g (2½ oz/¼ cup) tomato paste (concentrated purée)
400 g (14 oz) tin chopped tomatoes
12 okra, about 175 g (6 oz) in total, ends trimmed and chopped
400 g (14 oz/2 cups) basmati rice
125 g (4½ oz/½ cup) plain yoghurt
2 tablespoons pine nuts, toasted
1 large handful coriander (cilantro) sprigs

Combine the flour, cumin and coriander in a large bowl. Add the steak and toss until evenly coated. Add the onion, garlic, tomato paste and tomatoes and mix well. Season with sea salt and freshly ground black pepper.

Transfer the mixture to a slow cooker. Place the okra on top.

Cover and cook on low for 8 hours.

Meanwhile, near serving time, prepare the rice. Rinse the rice under cold running water until the water runs clear. Place the rice and 375 ml (13 fl oz/1½ cups) cold water in a large saucepan, then cover and cook over low heat for 20–25 minutes, or until the rice is tender.

Check the seasoning of the stew and adjust if required. Spoon the rice onto serving plates, then ladle the beef over the top. Add a dollop of yoghurt, sprinkle with the pine nuts, garnish with coriander and serve.

Preparation time: 15 minutes　　**Cooking time:** 8 hours　　**Serves:** 4–6

Preparation time: 30 minutes   **Cooking time:** 6 hours 30 minutes   **Serves:** 6

Lamb shanks braised with quince paste

1 onion, diced
2 garlic cloves, finely chopped
1 carrot, peeled and sliced
2 all-purpose potatoes, peeled
  and diced
90 g (3¼ oz/½ cup) dried apricots
180 g (6 oz/1 cup) pitted dates, halved
½ teaspoon mild paprika
½ teaspoon turmeric
½ teaspoon ground allspice
¼ teaspoon ground cardamom
100 g (3½ oz) quince paste, chopped
75 g (2½ oz/½ cup) plain
  (all-purpose) flour
6 French-trimmed lamb shanks
60 ml (2 fl oz/¼ cup) olive oil
80 ml (2½ fl oz/⅓ cup) red wine vinegar
1 litre (35 fl oz/4 cups) good-quality
  chicken stock
mashed potato, to serve (see page 134)
25 g (1 oz/¼ cup) toasted flaked
  almonds

Place the onion, garlic, carrot, potato, apricots, dates and ground spices in a slow cooker. Stir the quince paste through.

Spread the flour on a large flat plate and season well with sea salt and freshly ground black pepper. Dust the shanks in the flour, shaking off the excess.

Heat the olive oil in a large frying pan over medium–high heat. Add the shanks in batches and cook for 8 minutes, or until browned on all sides, turning occasionally. Remove each batch to the slow cooker, placing the shanks over the vegetables.

Add the vinegar to the frying pan and cook for 1–2 minutes, stirring to scrape up any cooked-on bits. Pour the sauce over the lamb shanks, then pour in the stock.

Cover and cook on low for 6 hours, or until the lamb is very tender and is falling away from the bone.

Serve on a bed of mashed potato, topped with the flaked almonds.

Quince paste is made by simmering peeled, cored and chopped quinces in sugar and water until the mixture becomes thick and jam-like. It is available in some supermarkets and specialty shops. Most commonly served with cheese, it provides a lovely sweet counterpart to the lamb in this dish. Instead of mashed potato, you could also serve the shanks with a creamy celeriac and potato mash — see our recipe on page 57.

Green curry of tofu and vegetables

Kaffir lime leaves are available from greengrocers or Asian supermarkets. They are sometimes just labelled 'lime leaves', and can be frozen for later use. To finish the soup, you could stir some Thai basil through it and garnish with some extra Thai basil sprigs or leaves. Alternatively, garnish the curry with long green chilli halves.

300 g (10½ oz) orange sweet potato, peeled and cut into 1 cm (½ inch) dice
8 baby corn
3 tablespoons green curry paste
500 ml (17 fl oz/2 cups) coconut cream
300 g (10½ oz) firm tofu, cut into 3 cm (1¼ inch) chunks
2 zucchini (courgettes), thickly sliced
60 g (2¼ oz) green beans, trimmed and cut into 3 cm (1¼ inch) lengths
250 g (9 oz/1 bunch) broccolini, washed and halved lengthways
1–2 tablespoons fish sauce
400 g (14 oz/2 cups) jasmine rice
2 tablespoons lime juice
6 kaffir lime leaves, finely shredded

Place the sweet potato and baby corn in a slow cooker. In a small bowl, whisk the curry paste and coconut cream until smooth, then pour over the vegetables.

Cover and cook on high for 2 hours, or until the sweet potato is tender.

Stir in the tofu, zucchini, beans, broccolini and 1 tablespoon of the fish sauce. Cover and cook for another 30 minutes, or until the green vegetables have softened.

Meanwhile, near serving time, prepare the rice. Rinse the rice under cold running water until the water runs clear. Place the rice in a saucepan with 450 ml (16 fl oz) water. Bring to the boil and boil for 1 minute. Cover tightly, reduce the heat to as low as possible and cook for 10 minutes. Remove from the heat and leave to stand, covered, for 10 minutes.

Stir the lime juice and half the lime leaves through the curry. Check the seasoning, adding another tablespoon of fish sauce if the curry needs more saltiness.

Ladle the curry into wide shallow serving bowls. Garnish with the remaining lime leaves and serve with the rice.

Preparation time: 15 minutes ❊ **Cooking time:** 2 hours 30 minutes ❊ **Serves:** 4

Preparation time: 20 minutes   **Cooking time:** 7 hours   **Serves:** 6

Lebanese lamb stew

2 tablespoons plain (all-purpose) flour
2 teaspoons sea salt
½ teaspoon freshly ground black
  pepper
1 tablespoon baharat
1.5 kg (3 lb 5 oz) lamb shoulder,
  trimmed and cut into 3 cm
  (1¼ inch) chunks
2 tablespoons tomato paste
  (concentrated purée)
125 ml (4 fl oz/½ cup) tomato passata
  (puréed tomatoes)
1 onion, finely chopped
2 garlic cloves, crushed
400 g (14 oz/2 cups) basmati rice
400 g (14 oz) tin white beans, rinsed
  and drained
1 handful coriander (cilantro) leaves
lemon cheeks, to serve
thinly shaved cucumber, to serve
baby English spinach leaves, to serve

Place the flour, salt, pepper and baharat in a large bowl. Add the lamb and toss until evenly coated, then place the lamb in a slow cooker.

Add the tomato paste, passata, onion, garlic, and 125 ml (4 fl oz/½ cup) water and stir until well combined. Clean the sides of the cooker with a damp cloth if necessary.

Cover and cook on low for 6–7 hours, or until the lamb is very tender and breaks apart when stirred.

Meanwhile, near serving time, prepare the rice. Rinse the rice under cold running water until the water runs clear. Place the rice and 375 ml (13 fl oz/1½ cups) cold water in a large saucepan, then cover and cook over low heat for 20–25 minutes, or until the rice is tender.

Add the white beans to the slow cooker and gently stir in. Cover and cook for a further 10 minutes to heat through.

Divide the lamb among serving bowls and garnish with the coriander. Serve with the rice, lemon cheeks, cucumber and baby spinach.

Baharat is a spice mixture used in Middle Eastern cooking. It is available in specialty stores and Middle Eastern supermarkets. Although there is no direct substitute, you can use any Middle Eastern spice mix in this stew. Instead of rice, you could also serve this stew with steamed couscous.

Moroccan fish tagine

1 red onion, sliced
8 new potatoes, scrubbed and cut in half
4 roma (plum) tomatoes, quartered
6 garlic cloves
1 red capsicum (pepper), trimmed, seeded and sliced
100 g (3½ oz) pitted black olives
125 ml (4 fl oz/½ cup) good-quality fish stock
a pinch of saffron threads
4 x 200 g (7 oz) firm white skinless fish fillets (such as ling)
2 tablespoons chopped preserved lemon rind
flat-leaf (Italian) parsley, to garnish
steamed couscous, to serve

Chermoula
1 tablespoon olive oil
2 garlic cloves, crushed
1 large handful coriander (cilantro) leaves, chopped
2 teaspoons ground cumin
2 teaspoons ground paprika
60 ml (2 fl oz/¼ cup) lemon juice
1 teaspoon sea salt

Place the onion, potato, tomatoes, garlic, capsicum and olives in a slow cooker.

Put all the chermoula ingredients in a small food processor and blend until a smooth paste forms. Mix 1 tablespoon of the chermoula into the stock until smooth, reserving the remainder for rubbing over the fish. Stir the saffron threads into the stock, then pour over the vegetables in the slow cooker. Mix well to combine.

Cover and cook on high for 3 hours, or until the potatoes are tender.

About 15 minutes before the vegetables are cooked, spread the remaining chermoula over both sides of each fish fillet and set aside for the flavours to be absorbed.

Add the fish to the slow cooker, then cover and cook for a further 30 minutes, or until the fish flakes when tested with a fork.

Stir the preserved lemon through the tagine. Garnish with parsley and serve with couscous.

✳ Preparation time: 20 minutes ✳ **Cooking time:** 3 hours 30 minutes ✳ **Serves:** 4

✳ Preparation time: 20 minutes ✳ **Cooking time:** 6 hours 30 minutes ✳ **Serves:** 4

African chicken

1 tablespoon olive oil
4 chicken drumsticks
4 chicken wings, wing tips removed and
   cut into two pieces at the joint
2 chicken thigh cutlets, quartered
2 onions, finely sliced
2 tablespoons berbere spice blend
2 garlic cloves, crushed
60 g (2¼ oz/¼ cup) tomato paste
   (concentrated purée)
400 g (14 oz) tin chopped tomatoes
coriander (cilantro) sprigs, to garnish
lemon cheeks, to serve

Herbed couscous
280 g (10 oz/1½ cups) instant
   couscous
1 small handful coriander (cilantro)
   leaves, chopped
1 tablespoon olive oil

Heat the olive oil in a large frying pan over medium–high heat. Brown the chicken pieces in batches for 5 minutes, or until golden all over, turning during cooking. Transfer each batch to a slow cooker.

Add the onion to the frying pan and cook, stirring occasionally, for 10 minutes, or until softened. Spread the onion over the chicken pieces in the slow cooker.

Add the berbere spice blend to the frying pan and cook for 1 minute, or until fragrant. Stir in the garlic and tomato paste and cook for 30 seconds. Add the tomatoes and cook, stirring, for 1 minute, or until heated through. Transfer the mixture to the slow cooker and gently mix through.

Cover and cook on high for 5–6 hours, or until the chicken is very tender. Season with sea salt to taste.

Meanwhile, near serving time, make the herbed couscous. Place the couscous in a heatproof bowl and pour in 375 ml (13 fl oz/ 1½ cups) boiling water. Cover with a tea towel (dish towel) and leave to stand for 5 minutes, or until the liquid is absorbed. Fluff the grains up with a fork, then stir in the coriander and olive oil. Season to taste with sea salt and freshly ground black pepper.

Spoon the couscous into wide shallow serving bowls. Arrange the chicken pieces over the top and drizzle with the sauce from the slow cooker. Garnish with coriander and serve with lemon cheeks.

Berbere is an African spice blend of salt, ground cumin, ground coriander, ground pepper, ajowan, fenugreek, allspice, ginger, chilli, nutmeg and cloves. You can buy it at specialty spice shops, but if you can't find it, use a Moroccan spice mix from the supermarket.

Thai chilli basil pork ribs

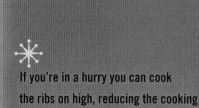

If you're in a hurry you can cook the ribs on high, reducing the cooking time to 4–5 hours.

250 ml (9 fl oz/1 cup) Thai sweet chilli sauce
2 tablespoons tomato sauce (ketchup)
2 tablespoons dry sherry
2 tablespoons fish sauce
2 garlic cloves, crushed
2 teaspoons grated fresh ginger
1.5–2 kg (3 lb 5 oz–4 lb 8 oz) American-style pork spare ribs
steamed rice, to serve
lime wedges, to serve (optional)

Apple salad
1 green apple, cored and cut into thick matchsticks
1 small handful coriander (cilantro) leaves
1 green chilli, seeded and sliced
2 teaspoons lime juice

In a large bowl, mix together the sweet chilli sauce, tomato sauce, sherry, fish sauce, garlic and ginger.

Cut the ribs into segments of two or three ribs per piece. Add them to the sweet chilli mixture and toss well to coat. Cover with plastic wrap and refrigerate overnight.

Transfer the ribs to a slow cooker. Pour the marinade mixture over the top.

Cover and cook on low for 8–10 hours, turning the ribs occasionally during cooking and basting them with the sauce.

Meanwhile, near serving time, make the apple salad. Place the ingredients in a small salad bowl and gently mix together.

Divide the ribs among serving plates and drizzle with the sauce from the slow cooker. Serve with the apple salad, steamed rice and lime wedges, if desired.

Preparation time: 10 minutes
plus overnight marinating

Cooking time: 10 hours

Serves: 4

✳ **Preparation time:** 20 minutes ✳ **Cooking time:** 6 hours 15 minutes ✳ **Serves:** 6

Five-spice caramel pork

1.3 kg (3 lb) pork belly rind,
  skin removed
1 tablespoon vegetable oil
55 g (2 oz/¼ cup) caster (superfine)
  sugar
1 teaspoon five-spice
1 star anise
250 ml (9 fl oz/1 cup) good-quality
  chicken stock
1 tablespoon fish sauce
185 ml (6 fl oz/¾ cup) light soy sauce
steamed white rice, to serve
sliced red chilli, to serve (optional)

Cucumber and ginger salad

1 Lebanese (short) cucumber, shaved
  lengthways into thin ribbons
1 spring onion (scallion), finely sliced
  on the diagonal
1 cm (½ inch) piece of fresh ginger,
  peeled and cut into thin matchsticks
1 tablespoon peanut oil
2 teaspoons rice vinegar

Cut the pork into 5 cm (2 inch) cubes. Heat the oil in a large frying pan over medium–high heat. Add one-third of the pork and fry for 5 minutes, or until golden, turning to brown all over. Transfer the pork to a slow cooker. Brown the remaining pork in two more batches, transferring each batch to the slow cooker.

Sprinkle the pork with the sugar and five-spice and gently mix to coat. Add the star anise, then pour in the stock, fish sauce and soy sauce.

Cover and cook on low for 6 hours, or until the pork is tender.

To make the cucumber and ginger salad, combine the cucumber, spring onion and ginger in a salad bowl. Whisk together the peanut oil and vinegar, pour over the salad and gently toss together.

Divide the pork among serving plates and drizzle with the cooking juices. Serve with steamed rice and the cucumber and ginger salad, sprinkled with sliced chilli if desired.

This dish originates from Vietnam, where it is known as 'thit heo kho tieu'. It is also delicious served with thick rice noodles.

Thai-style pumpkin soup

2 butternut pumpkins (squash), about 3 kg (6 lb 12 oz) in total, peeled, seeded and chopped
1 onion, finely chopped
2 kaffir lime leaves, torn
1 lemongrass stem, bruised
1 teaspoon finely grated fresh ginger
1 tablespoon fish sauce
270 ml (9½ fl oz) tin coconut cream
1 tablespoon mild red curry paste
875 ml (30 fl oz/3½ cups) good-quality chicken or vegetable stock
2 teaspoons lime juice
2 tablespoons Thai sweet chilli sauce
1 small handful coriander (cilantro) leaves
1 long red chilli, thinly sliced

Put the pumpkin and onion in a slow cooker with the lime leaves, lemongrass, ginger and fish sauce. Reserve 2 tablespoons of the coconut cream, then mix the curry paste with the remaining coconut cream until smooth. Pour over the pumpkin mixture, then pour in the stock and gently mix together.

Cover and cook on high for 3 hours, or until the pumpkin is tender. Set aside to cool slightly. Remove the lime leaves and lemongrass stem.

Working in batches, transfer the mixture to a food processor and blend until smooth. Stir in the lime juice and sweet chilli sauce and gently reheat if necessary.

Ladle the soup into serving bowls and drizzle with the reserved coconut cream. Serve garnished with the coriander and chilli.

Preparation time: 25 minutes   **Cooking time:** 3 hours   **Serves:** 4–6

✳ **Preparation time:** 25 minutes ✳ **Cooking time:** 4 hours 30 minutes ✳ **Serves:** 6

Moroccan ratatouille

80 ml (2½ fl oz/⅓ cup) olive oil,
  approximately
2 large red onions, cut into 2 cm
  (¾ inch) chunks
2 eggplants (aubergine), about 450 g
  (1 lb) each, trimmed and cut into
  2.5 cm (1 inch) chunks
2 large red capsicums (peppers),
  trimmed, seeded and chopped into
  2.5 cm (1 inch) chunks
2 tablespoons Moroccan spice mix
2 x 400 g (14 oz) tins chopped tomatoes
2 tablespoons tomato paste
  (concentrated purée)
400 g (14 oz) tin chickpeas, rinsed
  and drained
750 g (1 lb 10 oz) butternut pumpkin
  (squash), peeled, seeded and cut into
  3 cm (1¼ inch) chunks
2 tablespoons lemon juice
2½ teaspoons honey
110 g (3¾ oz/⅔ cup) pimento-stuffed
  green olives
2 tablespoons chopped coriander
  (cilantro)
250 g (9 oz/1 cup) Greek yoghurt
1 tablespoon chopped mint
steamed rice, to serve
harissa, to serve (see page 137)

Heat 1 tablespoon of the olive oil in a large heavy-based frying pan over medium heat. Add the onion and cook, tossing occasionally, for 4 minutes, or until the onion starts to soften and brown. Transfer the onion to a slow cooker.

Heat another 1 tablespoon of oil in the pan and add half the eggplant. Cook for 2 minutes on each side, or until the eggplant has softened slightly and is light golden, adding a little more oil as necessary. Add to the slow cooker.

Heat another tablespoon of oil in the pan, then cook the remaining eggplant in the same way. Add to the slow cooker.

Heat another tablespoon oil in the pan, then add the capsicum and cook for 3–4 minutes, or until it starts to soften and brown, turning often. Add the Moroccan spice mix and mix to combine well. Cook, stirring, for 30 seconds, or until fragrant, then add 1 tin of tomatoes, stirring to loosen any stuck-on bits from the bottom of the pan.

Transfer the mixture to the slow cooker. Add the remaining tomatoes, the tomato paste and the chickpeas and stir to combine well. Arrange the pumpkin on top of the mixture.

Cover and cook on low for 4 hours, or until the vegetables are very tender but still holding their shape.

Gently stir in the lemon juice, honey, olives and coriander. Season to taste with sea salt and freshly ground black pepper.

Combine the yoghurt and mint. Serve the ratatouille on a bed of steamed rice, with the minted yoghurt and harissa.

Chicken tikka masala

1.5 kg (3 lb 5 oz) chicken thigh fillets,
  trimmed of fat
2 x 400 g (14 oz) tins chopped
  tomatoes
1 large onion, finely diced
½ teaspoon ground chilli
½ teaspoon ground ginger
125 ml (4 fl oz/½ cup) thick cream
steamed rice, to serve
1 large handful chopped coriander
  (cilantro) leaves
mango chutney, to serve

Marinade
250 g (9 oz/1 cup) Greek yoghurt
2 tablespoons lemon juice
2 tablespoons tomato paste
  (concentrated purée)
5 garlic cloves, crushed
1 tablespoon grated fresh ginger
2 teaspoons ground cumin
2 teaspoons ground coriander
1 teaspoon garam masala
1 teaspoon ground turmeric
2 teaspoons sugar
1 teaspoon sea salt
½ teaspoon ground cardamom

Mint and chilli raita
4 tablespoons mint
2 garlic cloves, crushed
1 long green chilli, seeded and
  finely chopped
1 teaspoon ground cumin
250 g (9 oz/1 cup) Greek yoghurt

In a large bowl, mix together all the marinade ingredients. Add the chicken and toss to coat. Cover and refrigerate overnight, or for at least 6 hours.

Place the tomatoes, onion, chilli and ginger in a slow cooker and mix together. Add the chicken and pour the marinade over the top.

Cover and cook on low for 8 hours.

Meanwhile, near serving time, make the mint and chilli raita. Place the mint, garlic, chilli, cumin and 1 tablespoon of the yoghurt in a food processor and blend until smooth. Add the remaining yoghurt and process until just combined. Season to taste with sea salt and freshly ground black pepper and transfer to a small serving bowl.

Stir the cream through the curry. Serve the curry on a bed of rice, garnished with the coriander, with mango chutney and the mint and chilli raita to the side.

Preparation time: 20 minutes
plus at least 6 hours marinating

Cooking time: 8 hours

Serves: 6

Preparation time: 10 minutes   **Cooking time:** 4 hours   **Serves:** 4

Vegetarian chilli beans

1 onion, chopped
1 red capsicum (pepper), trimmed,
   seeded and chopped
400 g (14 oz) tin chopped tomatoes
2 x 400 g (14 oz) tins red kidney beans,
   rinsed and drained
1 tablespoon tomato paste
   (concentrated purée)
3 teaspoons ground coriander
2 teaspoons ground cumin
½ teaspoon chilli powder
2 garlic cloves, crushed
2 bay leaves
125 ml (4 fl oz/½ cup) good-quality
   chicken stock
400 g (14 oz/2 cups) basmati rice
90 g (3¼ oz/⅓ cup) sour cream
1 small handful coriander (cilantro)
   sprigs
flour tortillas, to serve

Avocado salsa
1 avocado, peeled and diced
2 tablespoons lemon juice
1 roma (plum) tomato, seeded and diced
½ red onion, thinly sliced

Place the onion, capsicum, tomatoes, beans, tomato paste, coriander, cumin, chilli powder, garlic and bay leaves in a slow cooker. Pour in the stock and stir to combine well.

Cover and cook for 4 hours on low.

Meanwhile, near serving time, prepare the rice. Rinse the rice under cold running water until the water runs clear. Place the rice and 375 ml (13 fl oz/1½ cups) cold water in a large saucepan, then cover and cook over low heat for 20–25 minutes, or until the rice is tender.

To make the avocado salsa, put all the ingredients in a bowl and stir to combine. Season to taste with sea salt and freshly ground black pepper. Cover and refrigerate until required.

Spoon the chilli beans into serving bowls. Top with a dollop of the sour cream and garnish with the coriander sprigs. Serve with the rice, avocado salsa and tortillas.

Chinese-style beef with cumin

1.25 kg (2 lb 12 oz) beef chuck
   steak, trimmed and cut into 4 cm
   (1½ inch) chunks
1 tablespoon julienned fresh ginger
2 garlic cloves, crushed
1 tablespoon caster (superfine) sugar
2 teaspoons ground cumin
1 tablespoon chilli bean paste
125 ml (4 fl oz/½ cup) Chinese rice wine
250 ml (9 fl oz/1 cup) good-quality
   beef stock
60 ml (2 fl oz/¼ cup) light soy sauce
400 g (14 oz/2 cups) jasmine rice
1 teaspoon sesame oil
1 Lebanese (short) cucumber, seeded
   and shredded
2 spring onions (scallions), cut into
   thin slivers
1 small handful coriander (cilantro)
   leaves

Put the beef in a slow cooker and scatter the ginger and garlic over. Sprinkle with the sugar and cumin. In a small bowl, mix together the chilli bean paste and rice wine. Pour over the beef, then pour in the stock and soy sauce. Gently stir to combine.

Cover and cook on low for 6 hours, or until the beef is tender.

Meanwhile, near serving time, prepare the rice. Rinse the rice under cold running water until the water runs clear. Place the rice in a saucepan with 450 ml (16 fl oz) water. Bring to the boil and boil for 1 minute. Cover tightly, reduce the heat to as low as possible and cook for 10 minutes. Remove from the heat and leave to stand, covered, for 10 minutes.

Stir the sesame oil into the beef mixture, then divide the beef among wide shallow serving bowls. Ladle the cooking juices over the top. Garnish with the cucumber, spring onion and coriander and serve with the rice.

Preparation time: 30 minutes   **Cooking time:** 4 hours 25 minutes   **Serves:** 6

Salmon tom kha

1.5 litres (52 fl oz/6 cups) good-quality
  chicken stock
4 x 185 g (6½ oz) salmon fillets,
  skin and pin bones removed
10 slices fresh galangal
4 large kaffir lime leaves, torn, plus extra
  shredded leaves, to garnish
2 x 400 ml (14 fl oz) tins coconut milk
2 tablespoons grated palm sugar
  (jaggery)
2 tablespoons fish sauce
175 g (6 oz) oyster mushrooms, sliced
4 small green chillies, split lengthways
80 ml (2½ fl oz/⅓ cup) lime juice
Thai basil leaves, to garnish

Lemongrass and galangal paste

2 lemongrass stems, white part only,
  finely sliced
5 cm (2 inch) piece of fresh galangal,
  peeled and finely chopped
4 coriander (cilantro) roots, washed well
  and chopped
5 red Asian shallots, peeled and chopped
4 garlic cloves, chopped
½ teaspoon white peppercorns
1–2 tablespoons vegetable oil, if needed

To make the lemongrass and galangal paste, put the lemongrass and galangal in a small food processor with the coriander root, shallot, garlic and peppercorns. Pulse until broken down and combined, adding the vegetable oil if needed to loosen the mixture.

Heat a small frying pan over medium heat. Add the lemongrass and galangal paste and cook for 1–2 minutes, or until fragrant. Transfer the paste to a slow cooker.

Slowly pour in the stock, mixing well. Add the salmon fillets, then scatter the galangal slices and lime leaves over the top.

Cover and cook on high for 4 hours.

Remove the salmon fillets and set aside for 10 minutes. When the fish is cool enough to handle, coarsely flake the flesh and set aside.

Stir the coconut milk, palm sugar and fish sauce into the broth in the slow cooker, mixing well. Return the salmon to the slow cooker and add the mushrooms, chilli and lime juice. Allow to heat through for a further 20 minutes.

Divide the salmon among deep serving bowls. Ladle the hot broth over the top and garnish with Thai basil and shredded lime leaves.

Similar in appearance to ginger, with a thin, pink-coloured skin, galangal is a fragrant rhizome used in South-East Asian cooking. You will find it in larger supermarkets and Asian grocery stores and will need a sharp, heavy knife to slice it. It is also available already sliced and dried.

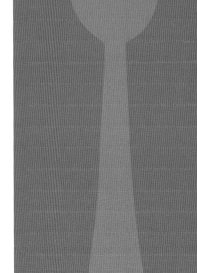

Yoghurt-marinated lamb with garlic and spices

We've served the lamb with a tomato and mint salad, made by tossing together 200 g (7 oz) halved grape tomatoes, 1 small handful mint leaves, 1 small handful coriander (cilantro) leaves and 1 small thinly sliced red onion.

2.5 kg (5 lb 8 oz) leg of lamb leg, fat trimmed
2 onions, quartered
1 cinnamon stick
1 litre (35 fl oz/4 cups) good-quality chicken stock
2 tablespoons cornflour (cornstarch)
2½ tablespoons chopped mint
naan bread, to serve
lemon cheeks, to serve

Yoghurt marinade
2½ teaspoons cumin seeds
10 green cardamom pods, seeds extracted
5 garlic cloves, chopped
finely grated rind of 1 lemon
2½ tablespoons lemon juice
1 teaspoon ground turmeric
½ teaspoon chilli flakes, or to taste
500 g (1 lb 2 oz/2 cups) Greek yoghurt
2 teaspoons freshly ground black pepper

Start by making the yoghurt marinade. Heat a small, heavy-based frying pan over low heat, add the cumin seeds and toast them without any oil, shaking the pan often, for 3–4 minutes, or until fragrant. Transfer to a mortar and pestle or electric spice grinder. Add the cardamom seeds and coarsely crush together. Tip the spice mixture into a small food processor. Add the garlic, lemon rind, lemon juice, turmeric and chilli flakes and process until the garlic is very finely chopped and the mixture is well combined. Scrape the mixture into a container large enough to fit the lamb. Add the yoghurt and pepper and mix together.

Using a small sharp knife, make deep incisions all over the lamb. Place the lamb in the container and turn to coat well in the yoghurt mixture. Cover the container with plastic wrap and refrigerate for at least 8 hours, or overnight.

Scrape as much of the yoghurt mixture from the lamb as possible, reserving the yoghurt mixture in the refrigerator.

Place the onion quarters in a slow cooker with the cinnamon stick. Place the lamb on top and pour in the stock. Season the lamb well with sea salt, then cover and cook on low for 6–8 hours, turning the lamb over halfway during cooking.

Near serving time, bring the reserved yoghurt mixture to room temperature.

Remove the lamb to a warmed platter; cover with foil and keep warm. Remove the onion using a slotted spoon and discard. Turn the slow cooker setting to high. Combine the cornflour with enough of the yoghurt mixture to make a smooth paste, then stir into the remaining yoghurt mixture. Whisk the yoghurt mixture into the liquid in the slow cooker. Cover and cook for 30–40 minutes, or until the liquid has thickened, whisking often to prevent lumps forming. Stir in the mint.

Tear the lamb into chunks. Serve drizzled with the yoghurt sauce, with naan bread, lemon cheeks and a salad.

Preparation time: 25 minutes
plus at least 8 hours marinating

Cooking time: 8 hours 45 minutes

Serves: 6

✳ **Preparation time:** 25 minutes ✳ **Cooking time:** 8 hours 20 minutes ✳ **Serves:** 4

Curried chicken and peanut soup

2 tablespoons fish sauce
2 garlic cloves, crushed
1 tablespoon lime juice
1 tablespoon soft brown sugar
2 small red chillies, seeded if desired, finely chopped
1.5 kg (3 lb 5 oz) chicken, rinsed
270 ml (9½ fl oz) tin coconut cream
250 g (9 oz) rice vermicelli noodles
chopped salted peanuts, to garnish
coriander (cilantro) sprigs, to garnish

Spice paste
1 small handful chopped coriander (cilantro)
½ small onion, chopped
3 spring onions (scallions), chopped
1 teaspoon grated fresh galangal
1 teaspoon ground turmeric
1 teaspoon ground coriander
2 tablespoons salted peanuts

Combine the fish sauce, garlic, lime juice, sugar and chilli in a slow cooker. Pour in 750 ml (26 fl oz/3 cups) water and stir until the sugar has dissolved. Add the chicken, placing it breast side down.

Cover and cook on low for 8 hours.

Put the spice paste ingredients in a food processor or blender with 2 tablespoons water. Process to a smooth paste.

Remove the chicken to a plate. Pour the cooking stock from the slow cooker through a sieve into the food processor, then blend with the spice paste until smooth. Return the stock to the slow cooker.

Discard the skin and bones of the chicken, then shred the meat using your fingers. Stir the shredded chicken through the soup with the coconut cream. Cover and cook for 20 minutes, or until heated through.

Meanwhile, place the noodles in a large heatproof bowl. Cover with boiling water and leave to soak for 10 minutes, or until softened.

Drain the noodles and divide among serving bowls. Ladle the soup over the top. Garnish with chopped peanuts and coriander sprigs and serve.

Prawn laksa lemak

Sambal oelek is a spicy condiment made from ground chillies. It is widely used in Indonesian and Malaysian cooking.

4 tablespoons laksa paste
540 ml (19 fl oz) coconut milk
1 tablespoon fish sauce
24 raw king prawns (shrimp), about 600 g (1 lb 5 oz) in total, peeled and deveined, tails left intact
300 g (10½ oz) rice stick noodles
1 cucumber
90 g (3¼ oz/1 cup) bean sprouts, tails trimmed
1 large handful coriander (cilantro) leaves
1 small handful Thai basil leaves
sambal oelek, to serve

In a small bowl, mix the laksa paste with the coconut milk. Pour into a slow cooker, then pour in the fish sauce and 500 ml (17 fl oz/2 cups) water. Add the prawns and gently mix.

Cover and cook on low for 2½ hours. Season to taste with sea salt.

Meanwhile, near serving time, place the noodles in a large heatproof bowl and cover with boiling water. Leave to soak for 20 minutes, or until softened.

Meanwhile, cut the cucumber in half lengthways and scrape out the seeds. Thinly slice the cucumber into matchsticks 5 cm (2 inches) long.

Drain the noodles and divide among deep serving bowls. Ladle the laksa over the noodles. Top with the bean sprouts, coriander and basil and serve with the cucumber and sambal oelek.

Preparation time: 15 minutes ✳ **Cooking time:** 2 hours 30 minutes ✳ **Serves:** 4

Preparation time: 20 minutes   **Cooking time:** 7 hours   **Serves:** 4

Vietnamese beef brisket

1.5 kg (3 lb 5 oz) beef brisket, cut into
    3 cm (1¼ inch) chunks
2 carrots, peeled and thinly sliced
2 lemongrass stems, white part only,
    chopped
2 long red chillies, seeded and sliced
    on the diagonal
10 cm (4 inch) piece of fresh ginger,
    peeled and cut into thin matchsticks
60 ml (2 fl oz/¼ cup) soy sauce
2 tablespoons fish sauce
2 tablespoons lime juice
400 g (14 oz/2 cups) jasmine rice
quartered cherry tomatoes, to garnish
90 g (3¼ oz/1 cup) bean sprouts,
    tails trimmed
1 handful Vietnamese mint, to garnish
1 small handful small basil leaves,
    to garnish

Place the beef, carrot, lemongrass, chilli, ginger, soy sauce and fish sauce in a slow cooker. Gently mix together.

Cover and cook for 6 hours on low.

Skim any fat from the surface of the sauce, then stir in the lime juice.

Turn the slow cooker heat up to high, then cover and cook for a further 1 hour.

Meanwhile, near serving time, prepare the rice. Rinse the rice under cold running water until the water runs clear. Place the rice in a saucepan with 450 ml (16 fl oz) water. Bring to the boil and boil for 1 minute. Cover tightly, reduce the heat to as low as possible and cook for 10 minutes. Remove from the heat and leave to stand, covered, for 10 minutes.

Spoon the rice into wide shallow serving bowls, then ladle the beef mixture over the top. Garnish with the cherry tomatoes, bean sprouts, mint and basil and serve.

This dish may also be served with rice noodles. Simply cover 300 g (10½ oz) dried rice noodles with boiling water and allow to soak for 5 minutes, or until softened, then drain and rinse. Before serving with the beef brisket, stir some chopped coriander (cilantro) through the noodles if desired.

Chicken and lentil curry

You can add a little more curry paste if you prefer a stronger flavour. You can use any flavoured curry paste for this dish.

10 skinless chicken thigh fillets, about 1 kg (2 lb 4 oz) in total
2 tablespoons Indian curry paste, such as madras
2 garlic cloves, finely chopped
2 teaspoons grated fresh ginger
1 long red chilli, seeded and finely chopped
8 spring onions (scallions), sliced on the diagonal
1 green capsicum (pepper), trimmed, seeded and sliced
350 g (12 oz) purple sweet potato, peeled and sliced on the diagonal into 3 cm (1¼ inch) chunks
400 g (14 oz) tin chopped tomatoes
125 ml (4 fl oz/½ cup) good-quality chicken stock
400 g (14 oz/2 cups) basmati rice
400 g (14 oz) tin green or brown lentils, rinsed and drained
coriander (cilantro) sprigs, to garnish
lime cheeks, to serve
Greek yoghurt, to serve

Trim the chicken thighs of excess fat and cut them into quarters.

In a large bowl, mix together the curry paste, garlic, ginger and chilli. Add the chicken and stir to thoroughly coat it in the spices. Cover and marinate in the refrigerator for 3 hours to develop the flavours.

Add the spring onion, capsicum, sweet potato, tomatoes and stock to the chicken mixture. Gently toss together, then transfer to a slow cooker.

Cover and cook on high for 4 hours, or until the chicken and sweet potato are tender.

Meanwhile, near serving time, prepare the rice. Rinse the rice under cold running water until the water runs clear. Place the rice and 375 ml (13 fl oz/1½ cups) cold water in a large saucepan, then cover and cook over low heat for 20–25 minutes, or until the rice is tender.

Meanwhile, add the lentils to the slow cooker and stir through the chicken mixture. Cover and cook for a further 10 minutes, or until the lentils are warmed through.

Spoon the rice into wide shallow serving bowls, then ladle the curry over the top. Garnish with coriander sprigs. Serve with lime cheeks and a small bowl of yoghurt.

Preparation time: 25 minutes
plus 3 hours marinating **Cooking time:** 4 hours 10 minutes **Serves:** 4

Preparation time: 15 minutes   **Cooking time:** 3 hours   **Serves:** 6

Sri Lankan fish curry

1 onion, cut into wedges
2 long green chillies, halved lengthways,
    then seeded and chopped
2 garlic cloves, finely chopped
1 tablespoon Indian curry powder
2 cm (¾ inch) piece of fresh ginger,
    peeled and cut into thin matchsticks
1 cinnamon stick
1 small handful curry leaves
2 teaspoons tamarind purée
400 ml (14 fl oz) tin coconut milk
125 ml (4 fl oz/½ cup) good-quality
    chicken or fish stock
900 g (2 lb) firm white fish fillets,
    such as ling
2 tablespoons lime juice
steamed rice, to serve
2 tomatoes, seeded and finely chopped,
    to garnish
coriander (cilantro) leaves, to garnish
lime wedges, to serve

Put the onion, chilli, garlic, curry powder, ginger, cinnamon stick and curry leaves in a slow cooker. Drizzle the tamarind purée over the top. Pour in the coconut milk and stock and mix together. Add the fish and gently mix to coat.

Cover and cook on low for 3 hours.

Stir the lime juice through the curry and season well with sea salt and freshly ground black pepper.

Serve on a bed of steamed rice, garnished with chopped tomato and coriander leaves, with lime wedges for squeezing over.

Chilli and anchovy lamb neck

For this recipe you could use 4 trimmed lamb shoulder chops instead of the neck chops.

1 onion, finely chopped
1 celery stalk, finely chopped
1 carrot, peeled and finely chopped
4 anchovy fillets, finely chopped
2 garlic cloves, finely chopped
1 large red chilli, chopped
2 kg (4 lb 8 oz) lamb neck chops, trimmed of excess fat and sinew
400 g (14 oz) tin chopped tomatoes
250 ml (9 fl oz/1 cup) good-quality chicken stock
125 ml (4 fl oz/½ cup) red wine
2 tablespoons finely chopped flat-leaf (Italian) parsley
steamed green beans, to serve

Mashed potato
800 g (1 lb 12 oz) spunta, sebago or coliban potatoes
40 g (1½ oz) butter, chopped
80 ml (2½ fl oz/⅓ cup) hot milk

Gremolata
1 handful flat-leaf (Italian) parsley, finely chopped
finely grated rind of 1 orange
1 small red chilli, seeded and finely chopped

Put half the onion, celery and carrot in a slow cooker.

In a small bowl, mix together the anchovy, garlic and chilli. Spread the mixture over both sides of the lamb chops. Season well with freshly ground black pepper.

Arrange the lamb chops in the slow cooker in a single layer. Scatter the rest of the vegetables over the top. Pour in the tomatoes, stock and wine.

Cover and cook on high for 6 hours, or until the lamb is tender.

Meanwhile, near serving time, make the mashed potato. Cook the potatoes in a large saucepan of boiling salted water for 20 minutes, or until very tender but not falling apart. Drain well, then return to the saucepan over low heat. Shake the pan gently until any remaining water evaporates. Using a potato masher, roughly mash the potatoes. Add the butter and hot milk and beat with a wooden spoon until fluffy. Season with sea salt and freshly ground black pepper.

Mix together the gremolata ingredients and set aside until needed.

Use tongs to remove the bones from the lamb chops if you wish. Divide the chops among serving plates and drizzle with the sauce from the slow cooker. Sprinkle with the gremolata and serve with the mashed potato and steamed green beans.

✳ **Preparation time:** 25 minutes   ✳ **Cooking time:** 6 hours   ✳ **Serves:** 4

❋ Preparation time: 25 minutes **❋ Cooking time:** 7 hours 20 minutes **❋ Serves:** 4–6

Chicken with harissa

2 kg (4 lb 8 oz) whole chicken
1 onion, peeled and halved
2 lemon zest strips
2 bay leaves
400 g (14 oz) tin chopped tomatoes
steamed couscous, to serve

Harissa

1 red capsicum (pepper), trimmed,
 seeded and cut into quarters
1 teaspoon chilli flakes, or to taste
1 tablespoon ground cumin
3 garlic cloves, crushed
1 tablespoon extra virgin olive oil

Start by making the harissa. Preheat the grill (broiler) to high. Place the capsicum on the grill tray, skin side up. Grill (broil) for 10 minutes, or until the skin blisters and blackens. Place the capsicum in a bowl and cover with plastic wrap. Leave to stand for 10 minutes, or until the capsicum is cool enough to handle. Peel the capsicum, discard the skin, then chop the flesh.

Place the capsicum in a small food processor with the chilli flakes, cumin and garlic. Blend until finely chopped. Add the olive oil and process until almost smooth. Season the harissa to taste with sea salt and freshly ground black pepper.

Wash the chicken and pat it dry with kitchen paper. Place half the onion, the lemon zest strips and bay leaves in the cavity of the chicken. Tie the legs together with kitchen string, then rub half the harissa over the chicken.

Finely chop the remaining onion and place it in a slow cooker with the tomatoes and remaining harissa. Gently mix together, then rest the chicken on top.

Cover and cook on low for 7 hours, or until the chicken is cooked through.

Remove the chicken to a warm platter and cover with foil to keep warm.

Transfer the sauce from the slow cooker to a small saucepan. Simmer over medium heat for 10 minutes, or until slightly reduced. Season to taste.

Carve the chicken and serve on a bed of couscous, generously drizzled with the sauce from the slow cooker.

We've served the chicken with a simple salad of halved yellow grape tomatoes, thinly sliced red onion and mint leaves.

Friends for dinner

Chicken madeira with mushrooms • Pork loin stuffed with prunes and walnuts • Braised lamb with celeriac and pinot • Octopus braised in red wine vinegar, red wine and oregano • Beef with creamy green peppercorn sauce • Chicken leg quarters with lemon and green olives • White bean and rocket soup with basil pesto • Lamb shanks with puy lentils • Osso buco with green olives • Chicken with caponata and balsamic vinegar • Boeuf en daube • Veal with tarragon lemon cream and broad beans • Slow-cooked fennel and rosemary-scented pork belly • Portuguese seafood stew • Chicken savoyarde • Navarin of lamb • Creamy beef with cherry tomatoes and sun-dried tomatoes • Braised pork with apples, apple cider vinegar and cream • Sauerbraten • Chicken galantine wrapped in prosciutto • Catalan beef stew with chocolate sauce • Veal with Jerusalem artichokes and mustard cream • Spanish beef with chorizo • Pork neck with star anise

✳ Preparation time: 15 minutes   **✳ Cooking time:** 6 hours 10 minutes   **✳ Serves:** 6

Chicken madeira with mushrooms

2 tablespoons plain (all-purpose) flour

1 kg (2 lb 4 oz) skinless chicken thigh
fillets, trimmed of fat, then halved

1 large leek, white part only, rinsed well
and chopped, plus extra leek slivers,
to garnish

2 teaspoons chopped rosemary

2 bay leaves

250 ml (9 fl oz/1 cup) good-quality
chicken stock

125 ml (4 fl oz/½ cup) madeira

20 g (¾ oz) butter

250 g (9 oz) button mushrooms, halved,
or quartered if large

125 ml (4 fl oz/½ cup) cream

1 small handful chopped flat-leaf
(Italian) parsley

lemon rind slivers, to garnish

mashed potato, to serve (see page 134)

Place the flour in a flat dish and season well with freshly ground black pepper. Add the chicken and toss well to coat, shaking off any excess.

Place the chicken in a slow cooker. Add the leek, rosemary and bay leaves, then pour in the stock and madeira. Gently mix together.

Cover and cook on low for 5 hours.

Melt the butter in a large frying pan. Add the mushrooms and cook for 5–10 minutes, or until golden, stirring occasionally. Add the mushrooms to the slow cooker, then stir in the cream.

Cover and cook for a further 1 hour, or until the sauce is thick. Stir the parsley through. Season the sauce with sea salt and freshly ground black pepper to taste.

Serve the chicken on a bed of mashed potato, drizzled with the sauce and garnished with leek and lemon rind slivers.

Pork loin stuffed with prunes and walnuts

1.5 kg (3 lb 5 oz) pork loin roast, rolled
375 ml (13 fl oz/1½ cups) good-quality chicken stock
1 tablespoon cornflour (cornstarch)
250 ml (9 fl oz/1 cup) cream
steamed greens, to serve
mashed potato, to serve (see page 134)

Prune and walnut stuffing
110 g (3¾ oz/½ cup) pitted prunes, chopped
4 dried figs, chopped
60 ml (2 fl oz/¼ cup) brandy
60 g (2¼ oz) butter
1 onion, finely diced
3 garlic cloves, crushed
120 g (4¼ oz/1½ cups) fresh breadcrumbs
2 tablespoons parsley, finely chopped
55 g (2 oz/½ cup) walnuts

To make the prune and walnut stuffing, place the prunes and figs in a small bowl, add the brandy and leave to soak for 20 minutes. Drain off the brandy, reserving 1 tablespoon.

Melt 20 g (¾ oz) of the butter in a small frying pan over medium–low heat. Add the onion and garlic and cook over low heat, stirring often, for 5 minutes, or until softened. Add another 20 g (¾ oz) of the butter to the pan and allow it to melt.

Transfer the onion and butter mixture to a small bowl. Add the prunes, figs, breadcrumbs, parsley and walnuts and mix well to combine.

Remove the string from the pork loin and pat the pork dry with kitchen paper. Place the pork on a clean surface, skin side down. Place the stuffing lengthways down the centre of the pork roast, making a sausage shape. Press down lightly. Fold the edge of the pork over and roll to enclose the filling. Secure the roll firmly with kitchen string, then season the pork with sea salt and freshly ground black pepper.

Melt the remaining butter in a large frying pan over medium–low heat. Add the pork and fry for 10 minutes, or until golden, turning to brown all sides.

Season the pork again, then place in a slow cooker. Pour in the stock and reserved brandy.

Cover and cook on high for 7 hours.

In a small bowl, mix the cornflour and cream until smooth. Stir the mixture into the sauce in the slow cooker. Cover and cook for a further 45 minutes, or until the sauce has thickened.

Carve the pork into six even slices and divide among serving plates. Spoon the sauce over. Serve with steamed greens and mashed potato.

Preparation time: 20 minutes
plus 20 minutes soaking

Cooking time: 8 hours

Serves: 6

Preparation time: 25 minutes **Cooking time:** 8 hours 45 minutes **Serves:** 4

Braised lamb with celeriac and pinot

630 g (1 lb 6 oz) celeriac, peeled and
    cut into 3 cm (1¼ inch) chunks
350 g (12 oz/1 bunch) baby carrots,
    scrubbed and trimmed
2 tablespoons olive oil
1 kg (2 lb 4 oz) boneless lamb leg,
    cut into 3 cm (1¼ inch) chunks
6 whole garlic cloves, crushed
750 ml (26 fl oz/3 cups) pinot noir
250 ml (9 fl oz/1 cup) good-quality
    chicken stock
2 bay leaves
1 tablespoon maple syrup
1 tablespoon caramelised balsamic
    vinegar
40 g (1½ oz) softened butter
2 tablespoons plain (all-purpose) flour
2 tablespoons chopped flat-leaf
    (Italian) parsley
steamed green beans, to serve
crusty bread, to serve

Place the celeriac and carrots in a slow cooker.

Heat the olive oil in a large frying pan over medium–high heat. Add the lamb in batches and fry for 5 minutes, turning to brown all over. Transfer each batch to the slow cooker.

Season the lamb with sea salt and freshly ground black pepper. Add the garlic, wine, stock, bay leaves, maple syrup and balsamic vinegar and gently mix together.

Cover and cook on low for 8 hours.

Mix the butter and flour together to make a smooth paste. Slowly stir the paste into the sauce in the slow cooker.

Remove the lid and cook for a further 30 minutes, or until the sauce has thickened.

Divide the braise among serving plates. Sprinkle with the parsley and serve with steamed green beans and crusty bread.

Caramelised balsamic vinegar is available from gourmet food stores, but if you can't find any, just use a combination of 1 tablespoon balsamic vinegar mixed with 1 teaspoon sugar. Buttered pasta noodles or risotto also go beautifully with this dish.

Octopus braised in red wine vinegar, red wine and oregano

2 large red onions, sliced
2 tablespoons lemon juice
1 garlic clove, crushed
2 bay leaves
2 teaspoons dried oregano
2 teaspoons brown sugar
1 teaspoon sea salt
60 ml (2 fl oz/¼ cup) red wine vinegar
60 ml (2 fl oz/¼ cup) red wine
16 baby octopus, cleaned
1 large handful chopped flat-leaf
   (Italian) parsley
2 tablespoons extra virgin olive oil

Spinach, orange and radish salad
4 radish, trimmed and thinly sliced
1 orange, peel and all white pith removed,
   cut into segments
1 handful baby English spinach leaves
2 tablespoons extra virgin olive oil
80 ml (2½ fl oz/⅓ cup) orange juice

Put the onion, lemon juice, garlic, bay leaves, oregano, sugar and sea salt in a slow cooker. Stir to dissolve the sugar. Pour in the vinegar, wine and 375 ml (13 fl oz/1½ cups) water.

Wash the octopus and pat dry with kitchen paper. Add to the slow cooker and gently mix together.

Cover and cook on low for 5 hours, or until it is easy to cut through the thickest part of the tentacles with a sharp knife.

Turn off the slow cooker, leave the lid on and allow to stand for a further 20 minutes, to allow the octopus to become very tender.

Meanwhile, make the spinach, orange and radish salad. Combine the radish, orange segments and spinach in a bowl. Whisk together the olive oil and orange juice and season to taste with sea salt and freshly ground black pepper. Pour over the salad and toss gently to combine.

Strain the octopus into a serving bowl. Add the parsley and olive oil. Season to taste, then mix together well. Serve with the spinach, radish and orange salad.

Preparation time: 20 minutes
plus 20 minutes standing

Cooking time: 5 hours

Serves: 4

Preparation time: 25 minutes ✳ **Cooking time:** 2 hours 5 minutes ✳ **Serves:** 4

Beef with creamy green peppercorn sauce

1 small onion, finely chopped

1 small carrot, peeled and finely chopped

1 celery stalk, finely chopped

2 garlic cloves, finely chopped

750 g (1 lb 10 oz) piece of beef fillet, trimmed of excess fat

8 thin slices of pancetta or streaky bacon, about 135 g (4¾ oz) in total

2 teaspoons olive oil

80 ml (2½ fl oz/⅓ cup) good-quality beef stock

80 ml (2½ fl oz/⅓ cup) red wine

30 g (1 oz) butter

1 tablespoon cornflour (cornstarch)

80 ml (2½ fl oz/⅓ cup) cream

55 g (2 oz) tinned green peppercorns, rinsed and drained

creamy celeriac and potato mash, to serve (see page 57)

steamed green beans, to serve

Put the onion, carrot, celery and garlic in a slow cooker.

Season the beef all over with freshly ground black pepper. Lay the pancetta slices on a clean work surface in a line next to each other, creating a sheet in which to wrap the beef. Place the beef fillet across the pancetta and fold the slices over to enclose the beef. Tie at intervals with kitchen string to secure the beef and pancetta.

Heat the olive oil in a large frying pan over high heat. Add the beef roll and fry for 5 minutes, or until the pancetta is golden brown, turning to brown all over. Place the beef in the slow cooker, nestled among the vegetables.

Place the frying pan back over the heat. Add the stock, wine and butter and stir to melt the butter. Bring briefly to the boil, then pour over the beef in the slow cooker.

Cover and cook on high for 1¾ hours, or until the beef is tender. Using tongs, remove the meat to a warm side plate. Remove the kitchen string, cover the beef with foil and leave to rest in a warm place while making the sauce.

Blend the cornflour with 1 tablespoon of water until smooth, then stir into the sauce in the slow cooker. Stir in the cream and peppercorns. Cover and cook for a further 10 minutes, or until the sauce has thickened a little.

Carve the meat into thick slices and arrange on serving plates. Spoon the peppercorn sauce over. Serve with creamy celeriac and potato mash and steamed green beans.

Chicken leg quarters with lemon and green olives

2 desiree potatoes, about 500 g
  (1 lb 2 oz) in total, peeled and cut
  into 2 cm (¾ inch) wedges
8 pickling onions or French shallots,
  peeled
8 chicken leg quarters
1 tablespoon olive oil
125 ml (4 fl oz/½ cup) white wine
2 tablespoons lemon juice
200 g (7 oz) green beans, trimmed
90 g (3¼ oz/½ cup) green olives,
  pitted
1 large handful flat-leaf (Italian)
  parsley, plus extra, to garnish
lemon wedges, to serve

Herb butter

60 g (2¼ oz) butter, softened
3 garlic cloves, crushed
1 tablespoon chopped lemon thyme
1 teaspoon chopped tarragon
60 ml (2 fl oz/¼ cup) lemon juice

Place the potato and onions in a slow cooker.

In a small bowl, mix together the herb butter ingredients until well combined. Use your fingers to gently loosen the skin away from the flesh of each chicken leg quarter, working as far down into the drumstick as you can. Ease the herb butter under the skin. Season the skin with sea salt and freshly ground black pepper.

Heat the olive oil in a large frying pan over medium heat. Add the chicken in batches, skin side down, and fry for 3 minutes, or until golden. Transfer each batch to the slow cooker.

Drain the fat from the frying pan. Add the wine to the pan and bring to the boil, using a wooden spoon to scrape up any stuck-on bits from the bottom of the pan. Add the lemon juice and cook for another 1–2 minutes, or until the liquid has reduced by half.

Pour the juices from the pan over the chicken in the slow cooker.

Cover and cook on low for 6 hours.

Turn the slow cooker heat to high. Add the beans, then cover and cook for a further 1 hour.

Stir the olives and parsley through. Divide the chicken and vegetables among serving plates. Scatter with extra parsley and serve with lemon wedges.

Preparation time: 25 minutes ✳ **Cooking time:** 7 hours 15 minutes ✳ **Serves:** 4

✳ **Preparation time:** 15 minutes   ✳ **Cooking time:** 8 hours 20 minutes   ✳ **Serves:** 6

White bean and rocket soup with basil pesto

1 large onion, chopped
2 garlic cloves, crushed
2 x 400 g (14 oz) tins cannellini beans,
   rinsed and drained
300 g (10½ oz/2 bunches) rocket
   (arugula), trimmed and chopped
2 litres (70 fl oz/8 cups) good-quality
   chicken stock
125 ml (4 fl oz/½ cup) cream
crusty bread, to serve

Basil pesto
2 tablespoons pine nuts, toasted
1 garlic clove, crushed
125 g (4½ oz/1 bunch) basil, leaves
   picked
35 g (1¼ oz/⅓ cup) grated parmesan
60 ml (2 fl oz/¼ cup) olive oil

Place the onion, garlic, beans, rocket and stock in a slow cooker. Gently mix until well combined.

Cover and cook on low for 8 hours.

Using a stick blender, process the soup until smooth, then stir the cream through.

Cover and cook for a further 20 minutes, or until warmed through.

Meanwhile, make the basil pesto. Place the pine nuts, garlic and basil in a food processor and blend until smooth and combined. Add the parmesan and process for a further 1 minute. With the motor running, add the olive oil in a slow steady stream until the pesto is smooth and of a sauce consistency. Season to taste with sea salt and freshly ground black pepper.

Ladle the soup into large serving bowls. Sprinkle generously with freshly ground black pepper. Add a generous dollop of the basil pesto and serve with crusty bread.

This soup can be frozen. Allow the soup to cool, then transfer to an airtight container. Label and date the container and freeze for up to 6 months. When making the pesto, toasting the pine nuts helps bring out their flavour. Gently fry them in a frying pan over medium–low heat, without any oil, for 3–4 minutes, or until golden brown, keeping a close eye on them and shaking the pan frequently so they don't burn.

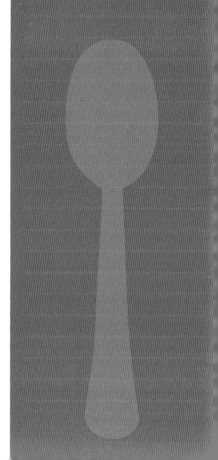

Lamb shanks with puy lentils

1 onion, chopped
1 celery stalk, chopped
1 carrot, peeled and chopped
1 parsnip, peeled and chopped
100 g (3½ oz) button mushrooms, halved
50 g (1¾ oz) pancetta or bacon, chopped
2 garlic cloves, chopped
2 anchovies, finely chopped
4 French-trimmed lamb shanks
250 ml (9 fl oz/1 cup) good-quality chicken stock
250 ml (9 fl oz/1 cup) red wine
200 g (7 oz/1 cup) puy lentils
1 tablespoon cornflour (cornstarch)
1 small handful flat-leaf (Italian) parsley, chopped
horseradish cream, to serve

Put the chopped vegetables and mushrooms in a slow cooker with the pancetta, garlic and anchovy. Gently mix together.

Arrange the shanks over the vegetables. Season well with sea salt and freshly ground black pepper, then pour the stock and wine over the shanks.

Cover and cook on high for 4 hours.

Place the lentils in a sieve and rinse under cold running water. Drain well.

Using tongs, turn the shanks in the cooking juices. Mix the lentils through the liquid, then cover and cook for a further 1 hour, or until the shanks and lentils are tender and cooked through.

Remove the shanks to a warm platter, cover with foil and keep in a warm place while finishing the sauce.

Blend the cornflour with 1 tablespoon water until smooth, then stir into the sauce and vegetables. Cover and cook for a further 15 minutes, or until the sauce has thickened slightly.

Serve the shanks on a bed of the lentils and vegetables. Garnish with the chopped parsley and serve with horseradish cream.

Preparation time: 25 minutes ☀ **Cooking time:** 8 hours 30 minutes ☀ **Serves:** 4–6

Osso buco with green olives

35 g (1¼ oz/¼ cup) plain (all-purpose) flour
8 beef osso buco, about 1.5 kg (3 lb 5 oz) in total
2 tablespoons olive oil
1 onion, finely chopped
1 celery stalk, finely chopped
1 carrot, peeled and finely chopped
400 g (14 oz) tin chopped tomatoes
2 bay leaves
2 rosemary sprigs
375 ml (13 fl oz/1½ cups) good-quality chicken stock
185 ml (6 fl oz/¾ cup) white wine
100 g (3½ oz/½ cup) green olives
3 tablespoons chopped flat-leaf (Italian) parsley, plus extra, to garnish

Soft polenta
500 ml (17 fl oz/2 cups) milk
150 g (5½ oz/1 cup) white or yellow polenta
40 g (1½ oz) butter
35 g (1¼ oz/⅓ cup) grated parmesan

Put the flour in a flat dish and season with sea salt and freshly ground black pepper. Dust the osso buco in the seasoned flour.

Heat the olive oil in a large frying pan over medium–high heat. Add the osso buco in batches and cook for 5 minutes on each side, or until golden brown all over, transferring each batch to a slow cooker.

Add the onion, celery, carrot, tomatoes, bay leaves and rosemary sprigs to the slow cooker, then pour in the stock and wine.

Cover and cook on low for 8 hours, or until the meat is very tender.

Meanwhile, near serving time, make the soft polenta. Put the milk in a saucepan with 250 ml (9 fl oz/1 cup) water and bring to the boil. Stirring continuously, add the polenta in a thin, steady stream. Cook over low heat, stirring often, for 30–35 minutes, or until the polenta is thick and soft. Remove from the heat and stir in the butter and parmesan.

Stir the olives and parsley through the osso buco mixture. Season to taste with sea salt and freshly ground black pepper.

Serve the osso buco on a bed of soft polenta, sprinkled with extra parsley.

Chicken with caponata and balsamic vinegar

2 tablespoons olive oil
3 anchovy fillets
2 red onions, thinly sliced
2 garlic cloves, crushed
1 red capsicum (pepper), trimmed,
   seeded and chopped into 1 cm
   (½ inch) pieces
1 yellow capsicum (pepper), trimmed,
   seeded and chopped into 1 cm
   (½ inch) pieces
2 eggplants (aubergine), cut into
   1 cm (½ inch) dice
100 g (3½ oz) pancetta, finely chopped
2 vine-ripened tomatoes, chopped
1 tablespoon baby capers, rinsed
   and drained
1 tablespoon balsamic vinegar
2 teaspoons sugar
1.5 kg (3 lb 5 oz) chicken thighs on
   the bone, skin removed and trimmed
   of any fat
1 small handful flat-leaf (Italian)
   parsley, chopped
steamed green beans, to serve

Heat half the olive oil in a large heavy-based saucepan over medium heat. Add the anchovies and onion and cook, stirring, for 3 minutes. Remove the onion mixture to a slow cooker.

Heat the remaining oil in the pan. Add the garlic, capsicum, eggplant and pancetta and sauté for 10–15 minutes, or until the vegetables are tender. Stir in the tomato, capers, vinegar and sugar and simmer for 3–5 minutes.

Transfer the caponata mixture to the slow cooker. Add the chicken and gently toss to coat well in the caponata. Clean the sides of the cooker with a damp cloth if necessary.

Cover and cook on low for 5–6 hours, or until the chicken is very tender. Season to taste with sea salt and freshly ground black pepper.

Transfer the mixture to serving plates and sprinkle with the parsley. Serve with steamed green beans.

✳ **Preparation time:** 30 minutes ✳ **Cooking time:** 6 hours 25 minutes ✳ **Serves:** 6

✳ **Preparation time:** 30 minutes ✳ **Cooking time:** 8 hours 25 minutes ✳ **Serves:** 4–6

Boeuf en daube

2 tablespoons olive oil

1 kg (2 lb 4 oz) beef chuck steak, cut into 3–4 cm (1¼–1½ inch) chunks

8 pickling onions, about 400 g (14 oz) in total, peeled and halved

150 g (5½ oz) bacon, cut into 1.5 cm (⅝ inch) pieces

1 carrot, peeled and chopped

1 celery stalk, chopped into 1.5 cm (⅝ inch) lengths

2 garlic cloves, crushed

1½ tablespoons plain (all-purpose) flour

1 tablespoon tomato paste (concentrated purée)

125 ml (4 fl oz/½ cup) good-quality beef stock

300 ml (10½ fl oz) red wine

1 tablespoon chopped thyme

2 bay leaves

400 g (14 oz) short pasta, such as casarecce, trofie or pasta twists

1 small handful chopped flat-leaf (Italian) parsley

crusty bread, to serve

Heat half the olive oil in a large heavy-based frying pan over high heat. Add one-third of the beef and fry for 5 minutes, or until golden, turning to brown all over. Transfer the beef to a slow cooker. Brown the remaining beef in two more batches, transferring each batch to the slow cooker.

Heat the remaining oil in the pan over medium–high heat. Add the onions, bacon, carrot and celery and cook, stirring, for 5 minutes, or until the vegetables are golden. Add the garlic and cook, stirring, for a further minute.

Stir in the flour and cook for 1 minute, or until smooth. Gradually add the tomato paste, stock, wine, thyme and bay leaves. Cook, stirring, for 3 minutes, or until the mixture boils and thickens. Pour the sauce over the beef in the slow cooker.

Cover and cook on low for 8 hours, or until the beef is very tender.

Meanwhile, near serving time, add the pasta to a large pot of rapidly boiling salted water and cook according to the packet instructions until al dente. Drain well.

Divide the pasta among wide, shallow serving bowls and spoon the beef mixture over the top. Sprinkle with the parsley and serve with crusty bread.

Boeuf en daube is a traditional French dish.

Veal with tarragon lemon cream and broad beans

To shell frozen broad beans, blanch them in boiling water for 1–2 minutes. Drain and rinse under cold water, then squeeze the beans out of their shells.

50 g (1¾ oz/⅓ cup) plain (all-purpose) flour
2 teaspoons sea salt
¼ teaspoon freshly ground black pepper
1.25 kg (2 lb 12 oz) veal stewing steak (blade or chuck), cut into 3 cm (1¼ inch) chunks
1½ tablespoons wholegrain mustard
125 ml (4 fl oz/½ cup) white wine
1 onion, very finely chopped
2 garlic cloves, crushed
2 tarragon sprigs, plus extra chopped leaves, to garnish
1 teaspoon grated lemon rind, plus extra strips, to garnish
60 ml (2 fl oz/¼ cup) cream
370 g (13 oz/2 cups) frozen or fresh broad (fava) beans, shelled
mashed potato, to serve (see page 134)

Combine the flour, sea salt and pepper in a large bowl. Add the veal and toss until evenly coated, shaking off any excess flour.

Transfer the veal to a slow cooker. Mix the mustard with the wine and add to the slow cooker along with the onion, garlic and tarragon sprigs. Gently mix together. Clean the sides of the cooker with a damp cloth if necessary.

Cover and cook on low for 4 hours.

Remove the tarragon sprigs and stir in the lemon rind and cream. Cover and cook for a further 1 hour, or until the veal is very tender.

Stir in the broad beans and cook for a further 15 minutes to heat through.

Ladle the veal into wide shallow serving bowls and generously spoon the sauce over. Garnish with extra lemon rind strips and chopped tarragon and serve with mashed potato.

Preparation time: 25 minutes ✳ **Cooking time:** 5 hours 15 minutes ✳ **Serves:** 6

Preparation time: 20 minutes　　**Cooking time:** 7 hours　　**Serves:** 4

Slow-cooked fennel and rosemary-scented pork belly

2 teaspoons fennel seeds, roughly
   crushed
2 teaspoons chopped rosemary
½–1 teaspoon chilli flakes
1 teaspoon sea salt flakes
½ teaspoon freshly ground black pepper
1 kg (2 lb 4 oz) pork belly, skin and rib
   bones removed
2 x 400 g (14 oz) tins butterbeans
   (lima beans), rinsed and drained
grated rind of 1 lemon
1 tablespoon lemon juice
1 tablespoon extra virgin olive oil

On a large plate, mix together the fennel seeds, rosemary, chilli flakes, sea salt and pepper. Roll the pork belly over the spice mix to crust it with the spices.

Place the pork belly in a slow cooker on a trivet, saucer or upturned cereal bowl.

Cover and cook on low for 5–7 hours, or until the pork is very tender. The pork will have a slight pink blush inside when perfectly cooked.

Remove the pork to a warm plate and cover with foil. Leave to rest in a warm place while finishing the sauce.

Skim the cooking juices from the slow cooker and reserve about 80 ml (2½ fl oz/⅓ cup).

Place the beans in a food processor with the lemon rind, lemon juice, olive oil and the reserved cooking juices, supplementing with a little stock or hot water if necessary. Purée for 4–5 minutes, or until smooth, scraping down the bowl with a spatula to mix well. Season to taste with sea salt and freshly ground black pepper.

Heat the bean purée in a small saucepan, stirring regularly, or covered in a microwave oven.

Serve the pork with the butterbean purée.

We've served the pork belly with a salad of cherry tomatoes and shaved fennel, garnished with fennel fronds. If you're in a hurry you can cook the pork on high, reducing the cooking time to 2½–3½ hours.

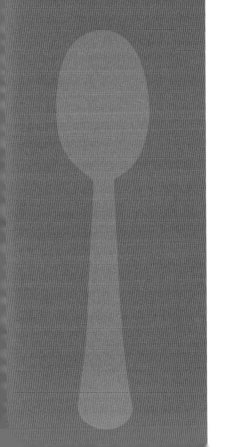

Portuguese seafood stew

¼ teaspoon saffron threads
1 leek, white part only, rinsed well and chopped into 1 cm (½ inch) pieces
1 chorizo sausage, halved and sliced
½ teaspoon smoked paprika
1 red capsicum (pepper), trimmed, seeded and chopped into 1.5 cm (⅝ inch) pieces
400 g (14 oz) tin chopped tomatoes
60 ml (2 fl oz/¼ cup) white wine
600 g (1 lb 5 oz) large raw king prawns (shrimp), peeled and deveined, leaving the tails intact
500 g (1 lb 2 oz) thick white fish fillets, chopped into 3–4 cm (1¼–1½ inch) chunks
2 tablespoons snipped chives
crusty bread, to serve
green salad, to serve

Place the saffron in a small bowl, cover with 1 tablespoon very hot water and leave to infuse for 10 minutes.

Put the leek, chorizo, paprika, capsicum, tomatoes and wine in a slow cooker. Add the saffron water and mix together well.

Cover and cook on low for 6 hours.

Add the prawns and fish, then cover and cook on high for a further 30 minutes, or until the prawns and fish are cooked through.

Ladle the stew into wide shallow serving bowls and sprinkle with the chives. Serve with crusty bread and a green salad.

Preparation time: 20 minutes   **Cooking time:** 6 hours 30 minutes   **Serves:** 4

☀ Preparation time: 20 minutes **☀ Cooking time:** 3 hours 35 minutes **☀ Serves:** 6

Chicken savoyarde

1 large onion, finely chopped
2 bay leaves
125 ml (4 fl oz/½ cup) good-quality
  chicken stock
125 ml (4 fl oz/½ cup) white wine
6 chicken breast fillets, about 1.25 kg
  (2 lb 12 oz) in total
250 ml (9 fl oz/1 cup) cream, at room
  temperature
1 tablespoon chopped tarragon
1 tablespoon dijon mustard
1½ tablespoons plain (all-purpose) flour
30 g (1 oz) butter, softened
100 g (3½ oz/¾ cup) grated gruyère
  cheese
40 g (1½ oz/1⅓ cups) ready-made
  mini-toasts
35 g (1¼ oz/⅓ cup) grated parmesan
2 tablespoons chopped flat-leaf (Italian)
  parsley
green salad, to serve
crusty bread, to serve

Combine the onion, bay leaves, stock and wine in a slow cooker. Place the chicken breasts on top in a single layer, then season with sea salt and freshly ground black pepper.

Cover and cook on low for 3 hours.

Remove the chicken from the slow cooker to a warm platter. Cover with foil and keep in a warm place while finishing the sauce.

Turn the slow cooker setting to high. Remove the bay leaves and stir in the cream, tarragon and mustard. Mix the flour and butter together in a small bowl, working them into a smooth paste. Whisking constantly, add the flour mixture to the liquid in the slow cooker.

Cover and cook for 30 minutes, or until the mixture has thickened, whisking often to prevent lumps forming.

Stir in the gruyère and season to taste with sea salt and freshly ground black pepper. Return the chicken to the sauce and heat briefly.

Finely chop the mini-toasts, then toss in a small bowl with the parmesan and parsley.

Divide the chicken among serving plates and drizzle generously with the sauce. Sprinkle the parmesan and parsley crumbs over the chicken and serve with a green salad and crusty bread.

This dish draws from the rich cuisine of the French alpine region, renowned for its fondue-style dishes.

Navarin of lamb

If baby vegetables are not available, just use larger vegetables, cut to the appropriate size. Navarin of lamb is also delicious served with our creamy celeriac and potato mash — see recipe on page 57.

35 g (1¼ oz/¼ cup) plain (all-purpose) flour
6 small French-trimmed lamb shanks, about 1 kg (2 lb 4 oz) in total
2 tablespoons olive oil
1 onion, finely chopped
2 garlic cloves, crushed
250 ml (9 fl oz/1 cup) white wine
250 ml (9 fl oz/1 cup) good-quality chicken stock
3 tablespoons tomato paste (concentrated purée)
12 new potatoes, scrubbed
12 small baby turnips, peeled
12 small pickling onions, trimmed and peeled
1 rosemary sprig
12 baby carrots, scrubbed
115 g (4 oz/¾ cup) frozen green peas, thawed
mashed potato, to serve (see page 134)

Spread 2 tablespoons of the flour on a plate and season with sea salt and freshly ground black pepper. Toss the lamb shanks in the flour to coat well; reserve the flour.

Heat the olive oil in a large frying pan. Add the shanks and fry for 5 minutes, turning to brown all over. Transfer to a slow cooker, then sprinkle with any reserved flour.

In a small bowl, mix together the onion, garlic, wine, stock and tomato paste, then pour over the shanks. Top with the potatoes, turnips, pickling onions and rosemary sprig.

Cover and cook on high for 4 hours.

Add the carrots, then cover and cook for a further 30 minutes, or until tender.

Remove the shanks and vegetables to a warm platter. Cover with foil and keep in a warm place while finishing the sauce.

Skim off any fat from the top of the sauce. Blend the remaining tablespoon of flour with 2 tablespoons water until smooth, then stir into the cooking liquid. Add the peas and cook for a further 10 minutes, or until the mixture has thickened slightly. Season to taste.

Return the vegetables and lamb to the sauce to heat through.

Serve on a bed of creamy mashed potato.

Preparation time: 25 minutes   **Cooking time:** 5 hours   **Serves:** 6

✳ Preparation time: 25 minutes ✳ **Cooking time:** 6 hours 30 minutes ✳ **Serves:** 6

Creamy beef with cherry tomatoes and sun-dried tomatoes

35 g (1¼ oz/¼ cup) plain (all-purpose) flour
2 teaspoons sea salt
½ teaspoon freshly ground black pepper
1 teaspoon sweet paprika
1.5 kg (3 lb 5 oz) beef chuck steak, trimmed of fat, then cut into 3 cm (1¼ inch) chunks
1½ tablespoons tomato paste (concentrated purée)
60 ml (2 fl oz/¼ cup) white wine
1 onion, finely chopped
2 garlic cloves, crushed
500 g (1 lb 2 oz) cherry tomatoes, halved
90 g (3¼ oz/½ cup) semi-dried (sun-blushed) tomatoes, chopped
250 g (9 oz/1 cup) sour cream
400 g (14 oz) fresh pappardelle
toasted pine nuts, for sprinkling
small basil leaves, to garnish
shaved parmesan, to serve

Place the flour, salt, pepper and paprika in a large bowl. Add the beef and toss until evenly coated. Shake off any excess flour, then place the beef in a slow cooker.

Mix the tomato paste with the wine, then add to the beef with the onion, garlic, cherry tomatoes and semi-dried tomatoes. Gently mix together. Clean the sides of the bowl with a damp cloth if necessary.

Cover and cook on low for 5–6 hours, or until the beef is very tender.

Stir in the sour cream, then cover and cook for another 30 minutes, or until heated through.

Meanwhile, near serving time, add the pasta to a large pot of rapidly boiling salted water and cook according to the packet instructions until al dente. Drain well.

Divide the pasta among serving bowls, then spoon the beef mixture over the top. Sprinkle with the pine nuts, scatter the basil leaves and parmesan over the top and serve.

Braised pork with apples, apple cider vinegar and cream

The braised pork is also wonderful served with roasted sweet potato wedges and lightly blanched cabbage dressed with butter.

1 kg (2 lb 4 oz) pork shoulder or neck, rolled and tied with kitchen string
1 tablespoon olive oil
2 whole garlic cloves
2 tablespoons apple cider vinegar
125 ml (4 fl oz/½ cup) good-quality chicken stock
4 apples, peeled, cored and cut into wedges
125 ml (4 fl oz/½ cup) cream
1 tablespoon finely snipped chives
steamed green vegetables, to serve
toasted flaked almonds, to garnish (optional)

Season the pork well with sea salt and freshly ground black pepper.

Heat the olive oil in a heavy-based saucepan. Add the pork roll and fry for 8–10 minutes, or until deeply golden on all sides, turning often.

Add the garlic to the pan, then pour in the vinegar and stock, stirring well with a wooden spoon to scrape up all the stuck-on bits from the bottom of the pan.

Transfer the pork and pan juices to a slow cooker. Cover and cook on high for 4–5 hours, or until the pork is tender.

Remove the pork to a warmed platter, cover with foil and leave to rest in a warm place while finishing the sauce.

Strain all the juices from the slow cooker through a fine sieve into a saucepan. Add the apples and cream and simmer, uncovered, for 5 minutes, or until the apples are tender.

Remove the apples and keep warm.

Simmer the sauce for another 5 minutes, or until it has reduced to the desired consistency.

Remove the string from the pork, carve the pork into thick slices and arrange on serving plates. Top with the apple wedges, drizzle with the sauce and sprinkle with the chives. Serve with steamed green vegetables, sprinkled with toasted flaked almonds if desired.

Preparation time: 15 minutes　　**Cooking time:** 5 hours 20 minutes　　**Serves:** 4

✳ Preparation time: 20 minutes
plus 1–2 days marinating **✳ Cooking time:** 8 hours 45 minutes **✳ Serves:** 8

Sauerbraten

1 small onion, halved, then sliced
6 cloves
3 bay leaves
1 teaspoon black peppercorns,
 lightly crushed
250 ml (9 fl oz/1 cup) red wine
125 ml (4 fl oz/½ cup) red wine vinegar
2.25 kg (5 lb) beef bolar blade,
 in one piece
2 tablespoons olive oil
35 g (1¼ oz/¼ cup) plain (all-purpose)
 flour
125 ml (4 fl oz/½ cup) good-quality
 beef stock
6 gingersnap biscuits
2 tablespoons soft brown sugar
lightly sautéed shredded cabbage,
 to serve
glazed baby carrots, to serve

Put the onion, cloves, bay leaves and peppercorns in a saucepan. Pour in the wine, vinegar and 250 ml (9 fl oz/1 cup) water. Bring to the boil over medium heat, then transfer to a large heatproof bowl and set aside to cool. Add the beef and turn to coat in the liquid. Cover and refrigerate for 1–2 days, turning the beef occasionally.

Heat half the olive oil in a large deep frying pan over medium–high heat. Drain the beef, reserving the marinade. Fry the beef for 10 minutes, turning to brown all over. Transfer to a slow cooker.

Heat the remaining oil in the pan. Add the flour and cook, stirring, for 2 minutes. Remove from the heat and slowly whisk in the stock and reserved marinade. Return to the heat and cook for 3 minutes, or until the sauce has thickened. Pour over the beef.

Cover and cook on low for 8 hours, or until the beef is very tender.

Add the biscuits and sugar to the sauce and cook for another 30 minutes, or until the biscuits are soft. Whisk to dissolve the biscuits, then season to taste with sea salt and freshly ground black pepper.

Carve the beef and divide among serving plates. Drizzle generously with the sauce and serve with sautéed cabbage and glazed baby carrots.

winter dish. The beef is ma... in red wine vinegar with vegetables and spices and then slow cooked. Ginger biscuits are added to the sauce for a sweet and spicy flavour.

Chicken galantine wrapped in prosciutto

10 g (¼ oz) dried porcini mushrooms
1 large double boneless chicken breast
   fillet, with tenderloins, about 725 g
   (1 lb 9 oz)
6 thin prosciutto slices, about 90 g
   (3¼ oz) in total
1 large handful baby English spinach
   leaves, about 30 g (1 oz)
2 tablespoons capers, drained
grated rind of ½ lemon
50 g (1¾ oz) butter
2 French shallots, finely chopped
2 garlic cloves, finely chopped
175 g (6 oz) mixed mushrooms,
   such as shiitake and Swiss brown,
   thickly sliced
60 ml (2 fl oz/¼ cup) white wine
1 tablespoon cornflour (cornstarch)
60 ml (2 fl oz/¼ cup) cream
roasted vegetables, to serve

Put the porcini in a small bowl, cover with 125 ml (4 fl oz/½ cup) hot water and leave to soak.

Remove the skin from the chicken and trim off any fat. Spread the two joined breasts out side by side on a chopping board, flesh side up. Without cutting through the join completely, make slits across the flesh to open the breast out, to more evenly distribute the flesh. Cover the chicken with a sheet of plastic wrap and pound gently with a mallet or rolling pin until the opened-out breast measures about 24 x 18 cm (9½ x 7 inches).

Lay the prosciutto slices on a board in a line next to and overlapping each other, creating a sheet to wrap the chicken in. Place the chicken fillet evenly over them, along the widest length.

Drain the porcini, reserving the soaking liquid, and chop. Lay the spinach over the chicken; scatter over half the porcini, the capers and lemon rind. Season well with freshly ground black pepper. Fold over to enclose the chicken, from the 18 cm (7 inch) shorter end. Tie with kitchen string to secure the chicken and prosciutto.

Melt half the butter in a large frying pan over high heat. Add the chicken roll and sear on all sides for 2–3 minutes, or until the prosciutto is golden brown. Put the chicken in the slow cooker.

Melt the remaining butter in the frying pan. Sauté the shallots, garlic and sliced mushrooms for 2–3 minutes. Add the wine, remaining porcini and the reserved porcini liquid and bring briefly to the boil. Pour over the chicken.

Cover and cook on high for 1¾ hours, or until the chicken and mushrooms are tender. Using tongs, remove the chicken roll to a warm side plate. Cut off the kitchen string, cover with foil and leave to rest in a warm place.

Blend the cornflour with 1 tablespoon water until smooth; stir into the sauce with the cream. Cover and cook for a further 15 minutes, or until the sauce has thickened a little.

Carve the chicken into 8 thick slices. Serve with the mushroom sauce and roasted vegetables.

✳ **Preparation time:** 30 minutes ✳ **Cooking time:** 2 hours 15 minutes ✳ **Serves:** 4

Preparation time: 20 minutes   **Cooking time:** 8 hours 15 minutes   **Serves:** 6

Catalan beef stew with chocolate sauce

75 g (2½ oz/½ cup) plain
  (all-purpose) flour
1 kg (2 lb 4 oz) beef chuck steak
  or stewing beef, cut into 2 cm
  (¾ inch) chunks
80 ml (2½ fl oz/⅓ cup) olive oil
185 ml (6 fl oz/¾ cup) red wine
2 large onions, chopped
1 carrot, peeled and diced
1 celery stalk, diced
1 leek, white part only, rinsed well
  and thickly sliced
4 garlic cloves, quartered
400 g (14 oz) tin chopped tomatoes
375 ml (13 fl oz/1½ cups) good-quality
  beef stock
60 g (2¼ oz/½ cup) grated good-quality
  dark chocolate
steamed rice, to serve
1 large handful chopped flat-leaf (Italian)
  parsley

Place the flour in a bowl and season with sea salt and freshly ground black pepper. Toss the beef in the flour to coat well, shaking off the excess.

Heat half the olive oil in a large frying pan over medium–high heat. Add half the beef and fry for 2–3 minutes, or until golden, turning to brown all over. Transfer the beef to a slow cooker. Add the remaining oil to the pan and brown the remaining beef. Place in the slow cooker.

Add the wine to the pan and cook, stirring, for 2 minutes, stirring with a wooden spoon to scrape up any stuck-on bits. Bring to the boil and allow to reduce by one-third. Remove from the heat and set aside.

Place the vegetables, garlic and tomatoes in the slow cooker and toss gently to mix. Pour in the wine mixture and stock.

Cover and cook on low for 7½ hours.

Stir the chocolate through the stew. Cover and cook for a further 30 minutes. Season to taste with sea salt and freshly ground black pepper.

Serve on a bed of steamed rice, sprinkled with the parsley.

Jerusalem artichokes are edible tubers belonging to the sunflower family. Not to be confused with ginger, which they resemble, they have a texture similar to potatoes and can be mashed, made into soups, or used as you would a root vegetable.

Veal with Jerusalem artichokes and mustard cream

50 g (1¾ oz/⅓ cup) plain (all-purpose) flour
1.5 kg (3 lb 5 oz) veal osso buco
60 ml (2 fl oz/¼ cup) olive oil
400 g (14 oz) Jerusalem artichokes, peeled and quartered
1 onion, thinly sliced
2 garlic cloves, crushed
60 ml (2 fl oz/¼ cup) verjuice or white wine
375 ml (13 fl oz/1½ cups) good-quality chicken stock
2 tablespoons chopped rosemary, plus extra, to garnish
2 tablespoons cream
1 tablespoon wholegrain mustard
soft polenta, to serve (see page 157)
lemon cheeks, to serve

Place half the flour in a bowl and season with sea salt and freshly ground black pepper. Toss the veal in the seasoned flour to coat well, shaking off the excess.

Heat half the olive oil in a large frying pan over medium–high heat. Add half the veal and fry for 5 minutes, or until golden, turning to brown all over. Transfer the veal to a slow cooker. Add the remaining veal to the pan and brown all over. Place in the slow cooker, then scatter the Jerusalem artichokes over the top.

Heat the remaining oil in the pan over medium heat. Add the onion and cook, stirring, for 5 minutes, or until golden. Add the garlic and cook for a further minute. Add the remaining flour and cook, stirring, for 2 minutes. Gradually stir in the verjuice and stock, then add the rosemary. Simmer for 3 minutes, or until slightly thickened. Pour the sauce over the veal.

Cover and cook on low for 7 hours, or until the veal is very tender.

Remove the veal from the slow cooker and place in a large bowl. Cover with foil and keep in a warm place while finishing the sauce.

Skim any fat from the surface of the sauce. Transfer the sauce to a small saucepan, then stir in the cream and mustard. Simmer over medium heat for 5 minutes, or until slightly thickened.

Serve the veal on a bed of polenta, drizzled with the sauce and sprinkled with extra rosemary. Serve with lemon cheeks for squeezing over.

Preparation time: 20 minutes **Cooking time:** 7 hours 30 minutes **Serves:** 4–6

✳ **Preparation time:** 10 minutes ✳ **Cooking time:** 6 hours 20 minutes ✳ **Serves:** 4

Spanish beef with chorizo

2 tablespoons extra virgin olive oil
1 kg (2 lb 4 oz) beef chuck steak,
    trimmed of fat and cut into 3 cm
    (1¼ inch) chunks
1 red onion, sliced
2 chorizo sausages, thickly sliced
2 garlic cloves, crushed
1 tablespoon smoked paprika
2 tablespoons tomato paste
    (concentrated purée)
2 x 400 g (14 oz) tins chopped tomatoes
1 red capsicum (pepper), trimmed,
    seeded and chopped into 3 cm
    (1¼ inch) chunks
sliced green chilli, to serve

Bean and orange salad
400 g (14 oz) tin borlotti beans,
    rinsed and drained
1 small red onion, thinly sliced
1 small handful flat-leaf (Italian) parsley
finely grated rind of 1 orange
1 orange
2 tablespoons olive oil
1 tablespoon dijon mustard

Heat the olive oil in a large heavy-based frying pan over medium–high heat. Add one-third of the beef and fry for 5 minutes, or until golden, turning to brown all over. Transfer the beef to a slow cooker. Brown the remaining beef in two more batches, transferring each batch to the slow cooker.

Add the onion and chorizo to the pan and cook, stirring, for 2–3 minutes. Add the garlic, paprika and tomato paste and cook for 1 minute. Stir in the tomatoes and capsicum, stirring to scrape up any cooked-on bits. Transfer the mixture to the slow cooker.

Cover and cook on high for 5–6 hours, or until the beef is very tender.

To make the bean and orange salad, combine the beans, onion, parsley and orange rind in a large bowl. Peel the orange, removing all the white pith. Holding the orange over a bowl to catch any juices, cut along each side of the white membranes to remove the segments. Add the orange segments to the bean mixture. Whisk the olive oil and mustard into the reserved orange juice and season to taste with sea salt and freshly ground black pepper. Pour the dressing over the salad and gently toss together.

Sprinkle the beef with the chilli. Serve with crusty bread and the bean and orange salad.

Spanish paprika is called pimenton and is available in both a sweet and a smoked variety. Here we are using the smoked variety. Both varieties are available from spice shops and most supermarkets. If you have more time you can cook the beef on low, increasing the cooking time to 8–10 hours.

Pork neck with star anise

1.5 kg (3 lb 5 oz) piece of pork neck
1 tablespoon olive oil
2 tablespoons soft brown sugar
2 bay leaves
1 cinnamon stick
4 cloves
2 star anise
500 ml (17 fl oz/2 cups) good-quality
   chicken stock
1 tablespoon cornflour (cornstarch)
mashed potato, to serve (see page 134)

Braised red cabbage
20 g (¾ oz) butter
1 tablespoon olive oil
1 granny smith apple, peeled,
   cored and thinly sliced
½ small red cabbage, finely shredded
60 ml (2 fl oz/¼ cup) apple juice
½ teaspoon caraway seeds (optional)

Season the pork with sea salt and freshly ground black pepper.

Heat the olive oil in a large frying pan over medium–high heat. Add the pork to the pan and cook, turning, for 10 minutes, or until browned all over. Transfer to a slow cooker. Sprinkle with the sugar, then add the bay leaves, cinnamon stick, cloves and star anise. Pour in the stock.

Cover and cook on low for 8 hours, or until the pork is tender.

Remove the pork to a warm platter. Cover with foil and keep in a warm place while finishing the sauce.

Blend the cornflour with 1 tablespoon water until smooth. Add to the sauce in the slow cooker and stir in well. Cover and cook for a further 15 minutes, or until the sauce has thickened.

Meanwhile, make the braised red cabbage. Heat the butter and olive oil in a large non-stick frying pan over medium heat. Add the apple and cook, turning often, for 3–4 minutes, or until light golden. Add the cabbage, apple juice and caraway seeds, if using. Cook, stirring, for another 5 minutes, or until the cabbage has just wilted. Season to taste.

Carve the pork into thick slices. Serve with the braised red cabbage and mashed potato.

✳ Preparation time: 10 minutes ✳ **Cooking time:** 8 hours 25 minutes ✳ **Serves:** 6

INDEX

Published in 2010 by Murdoch Books Pty Limited

Murdoch Books Australia
Pier 8/9
23 Hickson Road
Millers Point NSW 2000
Phone: +61 (0) 2 8220 2000
Fax: +61 (0) 2 8220 2558
www.murdochbooks.com.au

Murdoch Books UK Limited
Erico House, 6th Floor
93–99 Upper Richmond Road
Putney, London SW15 2TG
Phone: +44 (0) 20 8785 5995
Fax: +44 (0) 20 8785 5985
www.murdochbooks.co.uk

Publishing director: Kay Scarlett
Project editor: Kristin Buesing
Copy editor: Katri Hilden
Food editor: Leanne Kitchen
Cover concept: Yolande Gray
Design concept: Emilia Toia
Photographer: Natasha Milne
Stylist: Kate Brown
Food preparation: Kristin Buesing, Kirrily La Rosa
Recipes developed by Alison Adams, Tina Asher, Nick Banbury, Cynthia Black, Peta Dent, Michelle Earl, Nadia French, Leanne
  Kitchen, Kathy Knudsen, Michelle Lucia, Kim Meredith, Angela Tregonning and the Murdoch Books test kitchen.
Production: Joan Beal

National Library of Australia Cataloguing-in-Publication Data
Title: Slow cooker : throw it in and let it simmer
ISBN: 978-1-74196-446-2 (hbk.)
Series: My kitchen series.
Notes: Includes index.
Subjects: Electric cookery, Slow.
Dewey Number: 641.5884

A catalogue record for this book is available from the British Library.

PRINTED IN CHINA.

IMPORTANT:

Those who might be at risk from the effects of salmonella poisoning (the elderly, pregnant women, young children and those suffering
  from immune deficiency diseases) should consult their doctor with any concerns about eating raw eggs.

Never place meats that are still frozen, or partially frozen, in a slow cooker as this can cause food-poisoning bacteria to flourish;
  always have meat thawed fully before cooking. Also, never use the ceramic insert straight after it has been frozen or refrigerated as
  the sudden change in temperature could cause it to crack; always bring it back to room temperature first.